Defying Gravity

The Professional Edition
Breaking Barriers
The Triumphs of America's Top Female Entrepreneurs

Michele D Nalley, MS, NAR
American Real Estate Executive, Entrepreneur and Author

Defying Gravity

Copyright © 2024
All Rights Reserved
ISBN: 9798333060228

Acknowledgment

Writing this book has been a journey of exploration, learning, and growth, and it would not have been possible without the unwavering support and guidance of many remarkable individuals.

First and foremost, I want to express my deepest gratitude to my husband, Stephen Nalley. Your constant encouragement, wisdom, and love have been my bedrock throughout this entire process. Your profound insights into the world of real estate and affordable housing have greatly enriched the content of this book. Your patience and understanding during the long hours and countless drafts have been a source of immense strength. Stephen, your belief in my vision and your relentless pursuit of excellence have inspired me to push boundaries and strive for the highest standards.

To my family and friends, thank you for your endless support and for always believing in me. Your encouragement has been a driving force behind my dedication to this project.

I also extend my heartfelt thanks to my colleagues and mentors who provided invaluable feedback and guidance. Your expertise and perspectives have significantly shaped the depth and breadth of this book.

Lastly, to the readers of this book, thank you for your interest and engagement. It is my hope that this book serves as a valuable resource and inspires you to make a positive impact in the field of affordable housing.

With gratitude,

Michele Nalley

About the Author

Michele Nalley is an accomplished American real estate executive, entrepreneur, author, and the visionary founder and CEO of MKB Investment. With over 30 years of extensive experience in the real estate industry, Michele has held executive positions at some of the most prestigious real estate companies, including Inner Circle Capital, Black Briar Advisors, and The Orlando Housing Authority.

Michele's educational background is as impressive as her professional achievements. She holds a Bachelor of Science degree from the University of Central Florida and a Master's degree in Real Estate from Florida International University. Additionally, Michele is a licensed real estate professional in the state of Florida, further solidifying her expertise and commitment to the field.

As the Founder and CEO of MKB Investment, Michele has built and continues to manage a thriving real estate empire. Her company specializes in acquiring, managing, and profiting from rental properties, showcasing her adeptness in both strategic planning and hands-on property management.

In her book, The Real Estate Investor's Blueprint: Essential Steps for Acquiring, Managing, and Profiting from Rental Properties, Michele shares her wealth of knowledge and experience, providing invaluable insights and practical steps for both novice and seasoned investors. Her dedication to empowering others in the real estate industry shines through in her detailed guidance, making this book an essential resource for anyone looking to achieve success in property investment.

Preface

Breaking Barriers: The Triumphs of America's Top Female Entrepreneurs is a celebration of resilience, innovation, and visionary leadership. This book explores the journeys of remarkable women who have not only transformed their respective industries but have also paved the way for future generations of female entrepreneurs. These trailblazers have shattered glass ceilings, defied societal expectations, and driven substantial change through their unwavering determination and exceptional leadership.

Overview

The significance of female entrepreneurs in today's business landscape cannot be overstated. Women are increasingly taking on leadership roles, founding groundbreaking companies, and driving economic growth. Despite facing numerous challenges, these women have demonstrated extraordinary tenacity and creativity, making indelible marks on their industries. Breaking Barriers aims to shine a light on their stories, celebrating their achievements and extracting valuable lessons from their experiences.

Historical Context

The journey of women in business has been marked by persistent efforts to overcome deeply entrenched barriers. Historically, women were often relegated to supportive roles, with limited opportunities for leadership. However, the latter half of the 20th century saw a significant shift as women began to assert their presence in the business world, driven by changing social norms, legal reforms, and a growing emphasis on gender equality. The featured leaders in this book represent the pinnacle of this evolution, demonstrating that with determination and vision, women can excel in any domain.

Purpose of the Book

The primary goal of Breaking Barriers is to highlight the stories, achievements, and lessons from some of America's top female entrepreneurs. By delving into their biographies and examining their accomplishments, this book aims to provide inspiration and guidance for aspiring female leaders. Each chapter is dedicated to a different entrepreneur, offering a comprehensive look at their journey, the obstacles they overcame, and the unique contributions they have made to their industries.

Structure of the Book

This book is structured into twenty chapters, each focusing on a different female leader. The chapters are designed to provide a holistic view of each leader's background, career milestones, industry impact, and the lessons they impart. The final chapter, The Legacy of Female Business Leaders, serves as a conclusion, summarizing key lessons, identifying common themes, and offering a future outlook on the evolving role of women in business and entrepreneurship.

Breaking Barriers is not just a collection of biographies; it is a celebration of the spirit, resilience, and ingenuity of women who have defied expectations and reshaped industries. As you read through the chapters, you will not only learn about the incredible journeys of these leaders but also gain insights into the qualities and strategies that have driven their success.

This book is a testament to the power of female leadership and an inspiration for the next generation of women who aspire to make their mark in the world of business. By learning from the experiences and lessons of these trailblazers, we can continue to advance the cause of gender equality and create a more inclusive and equitable future for all.

Contents

Acknowledgment: ii
About the Author: iii
Preface: iv

Chapter 1: Introduction

- Overview: Introduction to the significance of female entrepreneurs in modern business.
- Historical Context: Evolution of women's roles in business and the challenges they have faced.
- Purpose of the Book: Highlighting the stories, achievements, and lessons from top female entrepreneurs.
- Structure of the Book: Explanation of the chapter layout and featured entrepreneurs.

Chapter 2: Estee Lauder - The Beauty Mogul

- Biography: Early life and career of Estee Lauder.
- Achievements: Founding and growing Estee Lauder Companies.
- Impact on Industry: Shaping the modern beauty industry.
- Lessons Learned: The importance of personal branding and product quality.

Chapter 3: Mary Kay Ash - The Direct Selling Pioneer

- Biography: Early life and career of Mary Kay Ash.

- Achievements: Founding Mary Kay Inc. and creating a successful direct selling model.
- Impact on Industry: Revolutionizing direct sales and women's entrepreneurship.
- Lessons Learned: Empowering others and building a strong network.

Chapter 4: Oprah Winfrey - The Media Powerhouse

- Biography: Oprah Winfrey's journey from poverty to media mogul.
- Achievements: Creating Harpo Productions and the Oprah Winfrey Network.
- Impact on Industry: Transforming television and media landscapes.
- Lessons Learned: Authenticity and the power of personal connection.

Chapter 5: Martha Stewart - The Domestic Diva

- Biography: Martha Stewart's early life and career in domestic arts.
- Achievements: Building Martha Stewart Living Omnimedia into a lifestyle empire.
- Impact on Industry: Shaping the modern lifestyle and home improvement sectors.
- Lessons Learned: Diversification and brand consistency.

Chapter 6: Meg Whitman - The E-Commerce Innovator

- Biography: Meg Whitman's background and rise in the tech industry.

- Achievements: Transforming eBay into a global e-commerce giant.
- Impact on Industry: Setting standards for online marketplaces.
- Lessons Learned: Strategic growth and adaptability.

Chapter 7: Sara Blakely - The Shapewear Visionary

- Biography: Sara Blakely's entrepreneurial journey and founding of Spanx.
- Achievements: Building Spanx into a multimillion-dollar brand.
- Impact on Industry: Revolutionizing the shapewear market and female entrepreneurship.
- Lessons Learned: Innovation and persistence.

Chapter 8: Indra Nooyi - The Corporate Strategist

- Biography: Indra Nooyi's path to becoming CEO of PepsiCo.
- Achievements: Driving growth and sustainability at PepsiCo.
- Impact on Industry: Advocating for corporate responsibility and health.
- Lessons Learned: Strategic vision and sustainable leadership.

Chapter 9: Angela Ahrendts - The Luxury Retail Leader

- Biography: Angela Ahrendts' career in fashion and technology.

- Achievements: Transforming Burberry and leading Apple's retail strategy.
- Impact on Industry: Bridging luxury retail with digital innovation.
- Lessons Learned: Brand revitalization and customer experience.

Chapter 10: Sheila Johnson - The Media Magnate

- Biography: Sheila Johnson's background and career in media.
- Achievements: Co-founding Black Entertainment Television (BET) and her ventures in sports and hospitality.
- Impact on Industry: Paving the way for African American media and entrepreneurship.
- Lessons Learned: Diversification and seizing opportunities.

Chapter 11: Safra Catz - The Tech Leader

- Biography: Safra Catz's journey in the technology sector.
- Achievements: Rising to become CEO of Oracle Corporation.
- Impact on Industry: Influencing corporate strategy and tech innovation.
- Lessons Learned: Strategic leadership and financial acumen.

Chapter 12: Lisa Su - The Semiconductor Pioneer

- Biography: Lisa Su's background and rise in the tech industry.

- Achievements: Leading AMD as CEO and transforming its fortunes.
- Impact on Industry: Shaping the future of semiconductors and computing.
- Lessons Learned: Innovation and resilience in technology.

Chapter 13: Rosalind Brewer - The Retail Trailblazer

- Biography: Rosalind Brewer's career in retail and leadership roles.
- Achievements: Leading as CEO of Walgreens Boots Alliance and Starbucks COO.
- Impact on Industry: Driving innovation and inclusion in retail.
- Lessons Learned: Strategic leadership and advocating for diversity.

Chapter 14: Conclusion - The Legacy of Female Business Leaders

- Summary: Recap of key lessons from each featured leader.
- Common Themes: Identifying recurring themes in their success stories.
- Future Outlook: The evolving role of women in business and entrepreneurship.
- Encouragement: Inspiring the next generation of female leaders.

Defying Gravity

Page Left Blank Intentionally

Chapter 1: Introduction

In the dynamic landscape of modern business, female entrepreneurs have emerged as pivotal forces driving innovation, economic growth, and societal transformation. Their influence spans across industries, redefining traditional business models and setting new benchmarks for success. Female entrepreneurs have proven that diversity in leadership brings unique perspectives and solutions, fostering environments that prioritize collaboration, social responsibility, and inclusivity.

The significance of female entrepreneurs is multifaceted. Economically, women-owned businesses contribute substantially to job creation and GDP growth. According to a 2019 report by American Express, women-owned businesses in the United States employed over 9 million people and generated $1.7 trillion in revenue. This economic impact underscores the critical role female entrepreneurs play in the national and global economy.

Beyond economic contributions, female entrepreneurs are often at the forefront of social change. They tend to champion causes such as gender equality, environmental sustainability, and community development. Their leadership styles, which frequently emphasize empathy, collaboration, and social impact, offer a refreshing contrast to traditional, profit-centric business models. This shift towards more holistic business practices is becoming increasingly relevant in today's world, where consumers and stakeholders demand ethical and sustainable operations.

Moreover, female entrepreneurs serve as powerful role models, inspiring a new generation of women to pursue their entrepreneurial aspirations. Their success stories provide tangible proof that women can excel in business, regardless of the barriers they may face. By breaking through glass ceilings and overcoming gender biases, these women pave the way for others to follow, fostering a culture of empowerment and ambition.

Despite these achievements, female entrepreneurs still encounter significant challenges. Gender biases, limited access to capital, and a lack of mentorship and support networks are among the hurdles they must overcome. However, their resilience and determination have led to substantial progress, proving that women are not only capable of thriving in business but are essential to its evolution and success.

Historical Context: Evolution of Women's Roles in Business and the Challenges They Have Faced

The journey of women in business has been marked by both significant progress and persistent challenges. Understanding this historical context is crucial to appreciating the strides female entrepreneurs have made and the barriers they continue to confront.

Early 20th Century: Restricted Roles and Emerging Opportunities

In the early 20th century, women's participation in the workforce was largely restricted to roles considered extensions of their domestic responsibilities, such as teaching, nursing, and clerical work. The prevailing societal norms dictated that a woman's primary duty was to her family, and professional ambitions were often discouraged.

However, the two World Wars catalyzed a shift in this paradigm. As men were drafted into military service, women were called upon to fill roles in factories, offices, and other sectors. This period demonstrated women's capabilities beyond traditional domestic roles, laying the groundwork for future advancements. Nevertheless, after the wars ended, women were expected to return to their previous domestic roles, and many did, but the seeds of change had been sown.

Mid 20th Century: The Women's Rights Movement and Legislative Progress

The mid-20th century saw the rise of the Women's Rights Movement, which significantly influenced women's roles in business. Activists advocated for gender equality, leading to landmark legislative changes. The Equal Pay Act of 1963 aimed to abolish wage disparity based on sex, and Title IX of the Education Amendments of 1972 prohibited gender discrimination in federally funded education programs, opening more opportunities for women in higher education and subsequently, in business.

Despite these legal advancements, women continued to face substantial barriers in the business world. Access to capital was a significant challenge, as financial institutions often hesitated to lend to female entrepreneurs. Additionally, women had limited access to professional networks and mentorship opportunities, which are critical for career advancement. Gender biases and stereotypes also persisted, creating an environment where women had to work harder to prove their capabilities.

Late 20th Century: The Rise of Female Entrepreneurs

The late 20th century marked a period of significant growth for female entrepreneurship. More women began to enter the business world, driven by both necessity and opportunity. The rise of dual-income households and the increasing cost of living motivated many women to seek additional income through entrepreneurship. Simultaneously, societal attitudes towards women in business began to shift, albeit slowly.

During this period, several influential female entrepreneurs emerged, breaking through barriers and setting new standards for success. Estee Lauder, Mary Kay Ash, and Martha Stewart are notable examples. These women built thriving businesses and became household names, demonstrating that women could excel in the entrepreneurial realm.

However, their journeys were not without challenges. They faced skepticism and resistance from male-dominated industries and often had to balance their professional ambitions with societal expectations around family and domestic responsibilities. Their success required resilience, creativity, and a willingness to challenge the status quo.

The Digital Age: New Opportunities and Persistent Challenges

The advent of the internet and digital technology in the late 20th and early 21st centuries brought new opportunities for female entrepreneurs. Online platforms democratized access to information and resources, enabling women to start and grow businesses with fewer barriers. Social media provided a powerful tool for marketing and networking, allowing female entrepreneurs to reach global audiences and connect with mentors, investors, and customers.

Despite these advancements, challenges remain. Women still face disparities in access to funding, with female-led startups receiving a smaller share of venture capital compared to their male counterparts. According to a 2020 report by PitchBook, female-founded companies received just 2.3% of venture capital funding in the United States. This funding gap reflects broader systemic issues, including gender biases within the investment community and the underrepresentation of women in leadership roles within venture capital firms.

Additionally, work-life balance continues to be a significant challenge for many female entrepreneurs. Societal expectations around gender roles often place disproportionate pressure on women to manage household and caregiving responsibilities, even as they pursue demanding professional careers. This "double burden" can limit their ability to dedicate time and resources to their businesses.

The Impact of Female Entrepreneurs

Despite these challenges, the impact of female entrepreneurs on modern business is profound. They have driven innovation, created jobs, and contributed to economic growth. Their leadership has introduced new business models that prioritize sustainability, social responsibility, and community impact. By challenging traditional norms and advocating for greater gender equality, female entrepreneurs have reshaped the business landscape and paved the way for future generations of women.

Key Milestones and Influential Figures

Throughout history, several key milestones and influential figures have played pivotal roles in advancing the cause of female entrepreneurship:

- Estee Lauder (1908-2004): A pioneer in the beauty industry, Estee Lauder founded her eponymous company in 1946. Through innovative marketing strategies and a commitment to quality, she built a global beauty empire and became a role model for aspiring female entrepreneurs.

- Mary Kay Ash (1918-2001): Founder of Mary Kay Inc., Ash revolutionized the direct selling industry by empowering women to achieve financial independence. Her emphasis on personal development and mentorship created a supportive community for women in business.

- Oprah Winfrey (1954-present): As a media mogul and philanthropist, Winfrey's influence extends far beyond her television career. She has used her platform to advocate for education, empowerment, and social justice, inspiring countless women to pursue their entrepreneurial dreams.

- Martha Stewart (1941-present): Stewart's success in lifestyle and media demonstrates the power of branding and diversification. Despite facing legal challenges, she rebuilt her empire and remains an influential figure in business.

- Madam C.J. Walker (1867-1919): Often considered the first female self-made millionaire in America, Walker built a successful business empire selling hair care products for African American women. Her legacy includes her contributions to philanthropy and social activism.

- Ruth Handler (1916-2002): Co-founder of Mattel and creator of the Barbie doll, Handler's innovation and marketing acumen transformed the toy industry. Barbie became an iconic brand, and Handler's success demonstrated the potential of female entrepreneurs in male-dominated industries.

Continued Progress and Future Outlook

The progress made by female entrepreneurs over the past century is significant, but there is still much work to be done. Efforts to address the gender funding gap, provide mentorship and support networks, and challenge societal norms around gender roles are critical to advancing the cause of female entrepreneurship.

Organizations and initiatives focused on supporting women in business are playing a vital role in this progress. Programs that provide access to funding, training, and mentorship are helping to level the playing field and create more opportunities for female entrepreneurs. Advocacy for policy changes that promote gender equality in the workplace is also essential to driving systemic change.

Looking ahead, the future of female entrepreneurship is bright. As societal attitudes continue to evolve and more resources become available, women will have greater opportunities to pursue their entrepreneurial aspirations. The rise of female entrepreneurs is not just a trend; it is a fundamental shift that is reshaping the business world for the better.

The significance of female entrepreneurs in modern business cannot be overstated. Their contributions to economic growth, innovation, and social change are profound and far-reaching. Understanding the historical context of women's roles in business and the challenges they have faced provides valuable insight into the progress that has been made and the work that remains.

By celebrating the achievements of top female entrepreneurs and highlighting the lessons learned from their journeys, this book aims to inspire and empower the next generation of women in business. The resilience, creativity, and determination demonstrated by these women serve as powerful reminders that success is achievable, regardless of the obstacles faced. As we continue to support and advocate for female entrepreneurs, we can build a more inclusive, innovative, and equitable business landscape for all.

Purpose of the Book: Highlighting the Stories, Achievements, and Lessons from Top Female Entrepreneurs

The purpose of this book is to celebrate the remarkable achievements of America's top female entrepreneurs who have redefined modern business and left an indelible mark on their industries. By sharing their stories, this book aims to highlight the diversity of experiences, challenges, and triumphs that these women have encountered on their journeys to success. Each of these entrepreneurs has navigated unique paths, overcoming barriers and seizing opportunities to build thriving enterprises. Their stories serve not only as a source of inspiration but also as a testament to the power of resilience, creativity, and determination.

Female entrepreneurs contribute significantly to the economy, innovation, and social change. Their impact extends beyond their individual businesses, influencing entire industries and communities. By celebrating their achievements, this book seeks to acknowledge their contributions and encourage recognition of the vital role women play in driving economic growth and innovation.

Inspiring Aspiration

One of the primary goals of this book is to inspire aspiring female entrepreneurs. The stories of these accomplished women demonstrate that success is attainable, regardless of the obstacles that may arise. By providing real-life examples of women who have built successful businesses from the ground up, the book aims to motivate readers to pursue their entrepreneurial dreams with confidence and conviction.

Aspiration is fueled by seeing role models who have achieved great things. This book offers a diverse array of role models, each with their unique approach to business and leadership. By showcasing these varied paths to success, the book emphasizes that there is no single formula for achieving one's goals. Instead, it highlights the importance of finding one's passion, leveraging strengths, and remaining adaptable in the face of challenges.

Offering Lessons

The journey of each featured entrepreneur is rich with valuable lessons that can benefit readers at various stages of their entrepreneurial endeavors. By distilling these lessons, the book provides practical advice and strategies that readers can apply to their own businesses. These lessons cover a wide range of topics, including leadership, innovation, branding, resilience, and strategic growth.

For example, Estee Lauder's story emphasizes the importance of personal branding and product quality. Mary Kay Ash's journey highlights the power of empowering others and building a strong network. Oprah Winfrey's success underscores the significance of authenticity and personal connection. By presenting these insights in the context of real-world experiences, the book offers actionable guidance that readers can implement to navigate their own entrepreneurial paths.

Promoting Diversity

Diversity and inclusion are critical components of a thriving business environment. The featured entrepreneurs in this book come from various backgrounds, industries, and experiences, demonstrating the value of diverse perspectives in driving innovation and growth. By showcasing the achievements of women from different walks of life, the book emphasizes the importance of diversity in fostering a more equitable and dynamic business landscape.

Promoting diversity involves recognizing and valuing the unique contributions that individuals from different backgrounds bring to the table. This book aims to highlight the diverse ways in which female entrepreneurs have succeeded, thereby encouraging a broader appreciation for the range of talents and perspectives that contribute to business success. By doing so, it seeks to inspire readers to embrace diversity in their own ventures and advocate for

inclusive practices within their organizations.
Encouraging Resilience

Resilience is a recurring theme in the stories of the featured entrepreneurs. Each of these women has faced significant challenges, setbacks, and moments of doubt. However, their ability to persevere and adapt in the face of adversity has been a key factor in their success. By highlighting their resilience, the book aims to encourage readers to develop their own capacity to overcome obstacles and remain steadfast in the pursuit of their goals.

Resilience is not just about bouncing back from failure; it is about learning from experiences, adapting strategies, and maintaining a positive outlook even in difficult times. The book provides numerous examples of how the featured entrepreneurs have demonstrated resilience, whether through innovative problem-solving, strategic pivots, or unwavering commitment to their vision. These stories serve as powerful reminders that setbacks are a natural part of the entrepreneurial journey and that success often comes to those who persist.

Structure of the Book: Explanation of the Chapter Layout and Featured Entrepreneurs

The book is structured into fourteen chapters, each dedicated to a prominent female entrepreneur who has made a significant impact on modern business. The chapters are organized to provide a comprehensive overview of each entrepreneur's journey, including their early life, career trajectory, major achievements, and the lessons learned along the way. This structure ensures that readers gain a holistic understanding of each entrepreneur's story while drawing valuable insights from their experiences.

Detailed Chapter Structure

Chapter 1: Introduction

The introduction sets the stage for the entire book, providing an overview of the significance of female entrepreneurs in modern business and the historical context of women's roles in the industry. It explains the purpose of the book and outlines the structure, giving readers a clear roadmap of what to expect.

Chapter 2: Estee Lauder - The Beauty Mogul

This chapter delves into the life and career of Estee Lauder, highlighting her journey from humble beginnings to founding one of the most iconic beauty brands in the world. It explores her innovative marketing strategies, her emphasis on product quality, and her impact on the beauty industry. The chapter concludes with key lessons from her story, emphasizing the importance of personal branding and maintaining high standards.

Chapter 3: Mary Kay Ash - The Direct Selling Pioneer

Mary Kay Ash's story is one of empowerment and innovation in the direct selling industry. This chapter covers her early life, the founding of Mary Kay Inc., and the revolutionary business model she created. It discusses her focus on empowering women and building a supportive network, as well as the significant impact she had on the industry. The lessons learned from her journey include the power of mentorship and the importance of creating opportunities for others.

Chapter 4: Oprah Winfrey - The Media Powerhouse

Oprah Winfrey's rise from poverty to becoming a media mogul is a story of resilience and authenticity. This chapter explores her early challenges, the creation of Harpo Productions, and the launch of the Oprah Winfrey Network. It examines how she transformed television and media landscapes, using her platform to inspire and uplift others. The chapter concludes with lessons on the importance of authenticity, personal connection, and leveraging one's influence for positive change.

Chapter 5: Martha Stewart - The Domestic Diva

Martha Stewart's journey from a model to a media and lifestyle mogul is a testament to diversification and brand consistency. This chapter covers her early career, the founding of Martha Stewart Living Omnimedia, and her influence on the modern lifestyle and home improvement sectors. It highlights her strategic use of branding and her ability to pivot and adapt in the face of challenges. The lessons from her story emphasize the importance of maintaining a consistent brand image and exploring multiple revenue streams.

Chapter 6: Meg Whitman - The E-Commerce Innovator

Meg Whitman's transformation of eBay into a global e-commerce giant showcases her strategic vision and adaptability. This chapter delves into her background, her tenure at eBay, and her subsequent roles in the tech industry. It discusses the standards she set for online marketplaces and her approach to scaling businesses. The lessons from her journey include the importance of strategic growth, innovation, and staying ahead of industry trends.

Chapter 7: Sara Blakely - The Shapewear Visionary

Sara Blakely's entrepreneurial journey, from selling fax machines to founding Spanx, is a story of innovation and persistence. This chapter explores her early life, the creation of Spanx, and how she built it into a multimillion-dollar brand. It highlights her unique approach to product development and marketing, as well as her impact on the shapewear market. The lessons learned from her story include the value of persistence, creativity, and staying true to one's vision.

Chapter 8: Indra Nooyi - The Corporate Strategist

Indra Nooyi's path to becoming the CEO of PepsiCo is marked by strategic vision and sustainable leadership. This chapter covers her early career, her rise through the ranks at PepsiCo, and her efforts to drive growth and sustainability. It examines her advocacy for corporate responsibility and her impact on the industry. The lessons from her journey include the importance of long-term planning, sustainability, and leading with integrity.

Chapter 9: Angela Ahrendts - The Luxury Retail Leader

Angela Ahrendts' transformation of Burberry and leadership at Apple highlight her ability to bridge luxury retail with digital innovation. This chapter explores her career in fashion and technology, her strategic initiatives at Burberry, and her role in revitalizing Apple's retail experience. It discusses her emphasis on brand revitalization and customer experience. The lessons from her story include the importance of innovation, customer-centric strategies, and brand evolution.

Chapter 10: Sheila Johnson - The Media Magnate

Sheila Johnson's journey from co-founding Black Entertainment Television (BET) to her ventures in sports and hospitality showcases her diversification and business acumen. This chapter delves into her background, the creation of BET, and her subsequent entrepreneurial endeavors. It highlights her impact on African American media and her approach to seizing opportunities. The lessons from her journey include the value of diversification, resilience, and leveraging one's success for broader impact.

Chapter 11: Safra Catz - The Tech Leader

Safra Catz's rise to become the CEO of Oracle Corporation underscores her strategic leadership and financial expertise. This chapter explores her journey in the technology sector, her contributions to Oracle's growth, and her influence on corporate strategy and innovation. It examines her leadership style and the challenges she faced. The lessons from her story include the importance of financial acumen, strategic thinking, and navigating complex business environments.

Chapter 12: Lisa Su - The Semiconductor Pioneer

Lisa Su's leadership at AMD and her transformation of the company highlight her innovation and resilience in technology. This chapter covers her background, her rise in the tech industry, and her efforts to turn AMD's fortunes around. It discusses her impact on the semiconductor industry and her approach to leadership. The lessons from her journey include the importance of innovation, resilience, and staying ahead of technological advancements.

Chapter 13: Rosalind Brewer - The Retail Trailblazer

Rosalind Brewer's career in retail and her leadership roles at Walgreens Boots Alliance and Starbucks demonstrate her strategic leadership and advocacy for diversity. This chapter explores her background, her contributions to retail innovation, and her efforts to drive inclusion in the workplace. It highlights her impact on the industry and her approach to leading large organizations. The lessons from her story include the value of strategic leadership, diversity, and fostering inclusive environments.

Chapter 14: Conclusion - The Legacy of Female Business Leaders

The conclusion recaps the key lessons from each featured leader, identifying common themes in their success stories. It provides a future outlook on the evolving role of women in business and entrepreneurship, emphasizing the importance of continued progress and support for female entrepreneurs. The chapter encourages readers to draw inspiration from the featured entrepreneurs and to pursue their own entrepreneurial aspirations with confidence and resilience.
Conclusion

By highlighting the stories, achievements, and lessons from top female entrepreneurs, this book aims to celebrate their contributions, inspire aspiring entrepreneurs, and promote a more inclusive and dynamic business landscape. The diverse experiences and insights shared in these chapters demonstrate that success is attainable, regardless of the obstacles faced, and that female entrepreneurs are integral to the continued evolution and growth of modern business.

Chapter 2: Estee Lauder - The Beauty Mogul

Estee Lauder, born Josephine Esther Mentzer on July 1, 1908, in Corona, Queens, New York, was the youngest of nine children in a family of Hungarian Jewish immigrants. Her parents, Rose and Max Mentzer, had left Hungary in search of better opportunities in America. From a young age, Estee exhibited a keen interest in beauty and skincare, influenced significantly by her uncle, Dr. John Schotz, a chemist who created creams and lotions in his small laboratory.

Growing up in a modest household, Estee was taught the values of hard work and perseverance. Her father ran a hardware store, where Estee spent many hours helping out. Despite the economic constraints, her mother emphasized the importance of personal grooming and appearance, instilling in Estee an appreciation for beauty that would later shape her career. Estee's mother believed in the transformative power of skincare and makeup, a belief that Estee adopted wholeheartedly.

Estee's first foray into the world of beauty began in her teenage years when she started helping her uncle with his business. She was fascinated by the process of creating creams and lotions and eagerly absorbed all the knowledge her uncle could impart. Estee began selling her uncle's products to her friends and neighbors, quickly realizing her natural talent for sales and marketing. Her charm, coupled with a genuine belief in the products, helped her build a loyal customer base.

After graduating from high school, Estee continued to refine her sales techniques and expand her knowledge of skincare. She would visit beauty salons and demonstrate her uncle's products, often giving out free samples to entice potential customers. Estee's entrepreneurial spirit and dedication to quality products laid the foundation for her future success.

In 1930, Estee married Joseph Lauder, a businessman who shared her ambitions and supported her entrepreneurial endeavors. The couple had two sons, Leonard and Ronald, and moved to Manhattan, where Estee began to dream of creating her own beauty empire. During the 1930s and 1940s, Estee continued to develop her skills and network, gaining valuable insights into the beauty industry. She recognized the potential for growth and innovation in a market that was still relatively nascent.

Achievements: Founding and Growing Estee Lauder Companies

Estee Lauder's journey from a young girl selling her uncle's skincare products to the founder of a global beauty empire is a testament to her vision, determination, and business acumen. In 1946, with a starting capital of $50,000, Estee and her husband officially founded the Estee Lauder Companies. Their first products included Super-Rich All-Purpose Creme, Creme Pack, Cleansing Oil, and Skin Lotion. Estee's hands-on approach and dedication to quality quickly set her products apart in the competitive beauty market.

One of Estee's most significant achievements was her innovative approach to marketing. She understood the power of personal connection and believed that the best way to sell a product was to get it into the hands of potential customers. Estee pioneered the use of free samples, a strategy that was revolutionary at the time. She would often give away samples to women at beauty salons, convinced that once they tried her products, they would become loyal customers. This approach not only boosted sales but also built a strong sense of trust and loyalty among consumers.

In 1948, Estee Lauder Companies secured its first major department store order from Saks Fifth Avenue in New York City. This milestone marked the beginning of the brand's expansion into high-end retail. Estee's relentless pursuit of perfection and her keen eye for detail ensured that her products met the highest standards. She personally oversaw the production process, from formulation to packaging, to maintain the quality that her brand promised.

The 1950s were a period of significant growth for Estee Lauder Companies. In 1953, Estee introduced Youth-Dew, a bath oil that doubled as a perfume. Youth-Dew was a game-changer, offering women a luxurious fragrance at an affordable price. It quickly became a best-seller and solidified Estee Lauder's reputation as a leader in the beauty industry. The success of Youth-Dew demonstrated Estee's ability to anticipate market trends and create products that resonated with consumers.

Defying Gravity

Throughout the 1960s and 1970s, Estee Lauder continued to innovate and expand her product line. She introduced several iconic products, including Re-Nutriv Cream, a luxurious skincare product that set new standards for anti-aging treatments. Estee also understood the importance of branding and created a distinctive image for her company, characterized by elegance, sophistication, and exclusivity.

Under Estee's leadership, the company expanded internationally, establishing a presence in major cities around the world. Estee Lauder Companies became synonymous with quality and luxury, attracting a global clientele. Estee's commitment to excellence and her ability to build strong relationships with retailers and customers were key factors in the company's international success.

In addition to her business acumen, Estee was a master of public relations. She cultivated a glamorous public persona and maintained close relationships with influential figures in the fashion and beauty industries. Estee's charm and charisma made her a beloved figure, and she leveraged her personal brand to promote her company's products. Her appearances at high-profile events and in the media helped to reinforce the image of Estee Lauder as a premier beauty brand.

The 1980s and 1990s saw further diversification and expansion of Estee Lauder Companies. Estee's son, Leonard Lauder, joined the company and played a crucial role in its growth. Together, they launched several new brands, including Clinique, Aramis, and

Prescriptives, each catering to different segments of the market. Estee's vision of a multi-brand strategy allowed the company to dominate various niches within the beauty industry.

Estee Lauder's impact extended beyond her own brand. She was a pioneer in promoting corporate social responsibility and philanthropy. Estee was a strong advocate for breast cancer awareness and research, and the company launched the Breast Cancer Awareness Campaign in 1992, which has since raised millions of dollars for research and education. Estee's commitment to giving back to the community and supporting important causes further solidified her legacy as a compassionate and visionary leader.

Estee Lauder's achievements have left an enduring legacy in the beauty industry. Her innovative marketing strategies, emphasis on quality, and ability to build a strong brand have set standards that continue to influence the industry today. Estee Lauder Companies remains a global leader in beauty, with a diverse portfolio of brands and products that continue to reflect Estee's vision and values.

Impact on Industry: Shaping the Modern Beauty Industry

Estee Lauder's impact on the beauty industry is profound and far-reaching. She pioneered many of the marketing and sales techniques that are now standard in the industry. Her emphasis on personalized customer service and the strategic use of free samples revolutionized how beauty products were marketed and sold.

Estee's vision extended beyond her own brand. She was instrumental in the creation of several iconic beauty brands under the Estee Lauder Companies umbrella, including Clinique, Aramis, and Prescriptives. Each brand catered to different segments of the market, allowing the company to dominate various niches within the beauty industry.

Estee Lauder's influence is also evident in the philanthropic efforts of the company. Estee herself was a strong advocate for breast cancer awareness and research, and the company has continued her legacy through initiatives like the Breast Cancer Awareness Campaign. This commitment to social responsibility has further solidified Estee Lauder Companies' reputation as a leader in the beauty industry.

Lessons Learned: The Importance of Personal Branding and Product Quality

Estee Lauder's journey offers valuable lessons for aspiring entrepreneurs. One of the key takeaways from her story is the importance of personal branding. Estee's hands-on approach and genuine belief in her products helped build a strong, personal connection with her customers. She understood that a brand is not just about products but also about the people behind it.

Another critical lesson is the emphasis on product quality. Estee was meticulous about the formulation and packaging of her products, ensuring that they met the highest standards. This commitment to quality not only set her products apart but also built trust and loyalty among her customers.

Estee Lauder's innovative marketing strategies also provide valuable insights. Her use of free samples and the "gift with purchase" concept were groundbreaking at the time and demonstrated the power of creative marketing. These strategies not only drove sales but also created a sense of value and exclusivity around her brand.

Estee Lauder's Lasting Legacy

Estee Lauder's contributions to the beauty industry and her innovative business practices have left a lasting legacy. The Estee Lauder Companies, which she founded and nurtured, continues to thrive and grow, remaining a dominant player in the global beauty market. Estee's pioneering spirit, dedication to quality, and innovative marketing techniques have set a benchmark for excellence in the industry.

Moreover, Estee Lauder's legacy extends beyond her business achievements. Her philanthropic efforts and commitment to social causes have had a lasting impact. The Estee Lauder Companies' Breast Cancer Awareness Campaign, launched in 1992, has raised millions of dollars for breast cancer research and education. Estee's dedication to giving back to the community and supporting important causes continues to inspire future generations of entrepreneurs and business leaders.

Estee Lauder's story is a testament to the power of vision, perseverance, and innovation. Her journey from a young girl selling her uncle's skincare products to the founder of a global beauty empire is an inspiration to aspiring entrepreneurs around the world. Estee's ability to anticipate market trends, create high-quality products, and build a strong brand has left an indelible mark on the beauty industry.

As the beauty industry continues to evolve, Estee Lauder's legacy remains a guiding light. Her emphasis on quality, innovation, and customer connection continues to influence the way beauty products are developed and marketed. The Estee Lauder Companies' commitment to excellence and social responsibility reflects the values that Estee herself embodied.

In conclusion, Estee Lauder's remarkable journey and achievements have forever changed the beauty industry. Her pioneering spirit, dedication to quality, and innovative marketing strategies have set a benchmark for excellence that continues to inspire and guide future generations of entrepreneurs. Estee Lauder's legacy is not only a testament to her vision and determination but also a powerful reminder of the impact that one individual can have on an entire industry.

Impact on Industry: Shaping the Modern Beauty Industry

Estee Lauder's influence on the modern beauty industry is undeniable, largely due to her transformative marketing strategies. She was a visionary who understood the power of direct customer engagement and personal connection long before these concepts became standard practice. Her innovative approach to marketing not only set her brand apart but also reshaped the way beauty products were sold and marketed globally.

One of Estee Lauder's most revolutionary strategies was her use of free samples. At a time when this practice was virtually unheard of, Estee Lauder saw the value in allowing potential customers to experience her products firsthand. She believed that if women tried her products, they would fall in love with them and become loyal customers. This simple yet effective strategy not only boosted sales but also built a strong, loyal customer base. Today, sampling is a common practice in the beauty industry, used by brands worldwide to attract and retain customers.

Another groundbreaking strategy was the "gift with purchase" concept. Estee Lauder introduced this idea in the 1950s, offering customers a free gift with a minimum purchase amount. This tactic not only increased sales but also created a sense of value and exclusivity around the brand. Customers felt they were getting more for their money, which encouraged repeat purchases and enhanced brand loyalty. The "gift with purchase" concept remains a staple in the beauty industry, demonstrating Estee Lauder's lasting influence on marketing practices.

Estee Lauder also understood the importance of creating an aspirational brand image. She positioned her products as luxury items that every woman could afford, effectively democratizing the luxury beauty market. Her elegant packaging, sophisticated advertising campaigns, and association with high-profile figures and events helped to create a prestigious image for her brand. Estee Lauder's ability to blend luxury with accessibility set a new standard in the beauty industry, inspiring countless brands to follow suit.

Pioneering Personalized Customer Service

Estee Lauder's commitment to personalized customer service was another key factor in her success and influence. She believed that building personal relationships with customers was essential for brand loyalty. Estee Lauder herself would often visit department stores and beauty counters, engaging directly with customers and demonstrating her products. Her personal touch and genuine interest in her customers' needs created a strong emotional connection to the brand.

This emphasis on personalized service extended to her company's business model. Estee Lauder trained her beauty advisors to provide individualized consultations, helping customers choose the right products for their skin types and beauty needs. This approach not only enhanced the customer experience but also positioned Estee Lauder as a trusted advisor in beauty, rather than just a product supplier. Personalized service became a hallmark of the Estee Lauder brand, setting a new standard for the industry.

In today's beauty market, personalized service and customization are more important than ever. Advances in technology have enabled brands to offer highly personalized experiences, from customized skincare regimens to personalized product recommendations based on data analytics. Estee Lauder's early commitment to personalized service laid the groundwork for these modern practices, demonstrating her foresight and understanding of customer needs.

Expansion of Product Lines and Market Segments

Estee Lauder's vision extended beyond individual products to the creation of a diversified portfolio of brands that catered to different market segments. She recognized that the beauty industry had diverse customer needs and preferences, and she sought to address these through targeted brand development.

In 1968, Estee Lauder launched Clinique, a dermatologist-developed skincare and cosmetics line that catered to consumers with sensitive skin and specific dermatological needs. Clinique's success was due in part to its unique approach to skincare, which emphasized hypoallergenic and fragrance-free products. Clinique's clean, clinical branding and focus on efficacy resonated with consumers, establishing it as a leader in the skincare market. This strategic expansion allowed Estee Lauder Companies to reach a broader audience and reinforce its reputation for innovation and quality.

Another notable expansion was the acquisition of Aramis in 1964, which marked Estee Lauder's entry into the men's grooming market. Recognizing the untapped potential in men's skincare and fragrance, Estee Lauder developed Aramis into a successful brand that addressed the grooming needs of men.

This move not only diversified the company's product offerings but also demonstrated Estee Lauder's ability to anticipate market trends and capitalize on emerging opportunities.

The introduction of brands like Prescriptives, Origins, and Aveda further exemplified Estee Lauder's commitment to innovation and market segmentation. Each brand was designed to address specific consumer needs and preferences, from customizable makeup solutions to natural and organic skincare products. This multi-brand strategy allowed Estee Lauder Companies to dominate various niches within the beauty industry, setting a precedent for other beauty conglomerates.

Global Expansion and International Influence

Estee Lauder's impact on the beauty industry extended far beyond the United States. She recognized the potential for international growth early on and pursued an aggressive global expansion strategy. By the 1960s, Estee Lauder products were available in major cities around the world, from London and Paris to Tokyo and Hong Kong.

Estee Lauder's approach to international expansion was strategic and thoughtful. She ensured that her products and marketing campaigns were tailored to the cultural and aesthetic preferences of each market. This localization strategy helped to establish the Estee Lauder brand as a global leader in beauty, respected and loved by consumers worldwide.
Today, Estee Lauder Companies operates in over 150 countries, with a diverse portfolio of brands that cater

to a global audience. The company's success in international markets is a testament to Estee Lauder's vision and strategic foresight. Her ability to build a global brand without compromising on quality or customer experience set a new standard for international business expansion in the beauty industry.

Commitment to Corporate Social Responsibility

Estee Lauder was a pioneer in promoting corporate social responsibility (CSR) long before it became a common practice in the business world. She believed that businesses had a responsibility to give back to society and support important causes. This commitment to CSR is evident in the Estee Lauder Companies' long-standing support for breast cancer awareness and research.

In 1992, Evelyn H. Lauder, Estee Lauder's daughter-in-law, co-created the pink ribbon, a symbol of breast cancer awareness, and launched the Breast Cancer Awareness Campaign. This initiative has since raised millions of dollars for breast cancer research and education, and has helped to increase awareness and early detection of the disease. Estee Lauder Companies' commitment to this cause reflects the values and principles that Estee herself championed.

The company's CSR initiatives extend beyond breast cancer awareness. Estee Lauder Companies is also committed to environmental sustainability, ethical sourcing, and community support. These efforts align with the growing consumer demand for socially responsible and sustainable business practices. Estee Lauder's early recognition of the importance of CSR has had a lasting impact on the industry, influencing other brands to adopt similar initiatives and prioritize social and environmental responsibility.

Lessons Learned: The Importance of Personal Branding and Product Quality

Estee Lauder's success can be attributed in large part to her mastery of personal branding. She understood that a strong personal brand could create a powerful connection with consumers and differentiate her products in a crowded market. Estee's personal brand was synonymous with elegance, sophistication, and quality, and she leveraged this image to build a loyal customer base and establish her company as a leader in the beauty industry.

One of the key elements of Estee's personal branding strategy was her hands-on approach. She was actively involved in every aspect of her business, from product development to marketing and sales. Estee's personal touch and attention to detail ensured that her products met the highest standards and reflected her values. This level of involvement also helped to build trust and credibility with customers, who appreciated her commitment to quality and excellence.

Estee Lauder's personal brand was also characterized by her glamorous public persona. She cultivated a sophisticated image through her appearances at high-profile events, media interviews, and elegant advertising campaigns. Estee's ability to blend her personal style with her business brand created a sense of aspiration and allure around her products. Customers were not just buying beauty products; they were buying into the Estee Lauder lifestyle.

In today's business world, personal branding remains a critical component of success. Entrepreneurs and business leaders can learn from Estee Lauder's example by building strong, authentic personal brands that resonate with their target audience. Personal branding is not just about self-promotion; it is about conveying your values, vision, and unique qualities in a way that connects with others and builds trust.

The Importance of Product Quality

Another fundamental lesson from Estee Lauder's journey is the importance of product quality. Estee was unwavering in her commitment to creating high-quality products that delivered on their promises. She believed that the best marketing in the world could not compensate for a subpar product, and she made quality the cornerstone of her brand.

Estee Lauder's dedication to quality was evident in every aspect of her products, from formulation to packaging. She worked closely with chemists and product developers to ensure that her skincare and makeup products met the highest standards of efficacy and safety. Estee also paid meticulous attention to packaging, understanding that the presentation of a product could enhance its perceived value and appeal.

This focus on quality helped to differentiate Estee

Lauder products in a competitive market. Customers knew that when they purchased an Estee Lauder product, they were getting something that was carefully crafted and rigorously tested. This reputation for quality built trust and loyalty, driving repeat purchases and word-of-mouth recommendations.

In addition to product quality, Estee Lauder understood the importance of continuous innovation. She was constantly looking for ways to improve her products and introduce new offerings that met the evolving needs of her customers. This commitment to innovation ensured that Estee Lauder stayed at the forefront of the beauty industry and maintained its competitive edge.

For modern entrepreneurs, the lesson is clear: product quality should never be compromised. Investing in high-quality ingredients, rigorous testing, and thoughtful design can set a brand apart and build lasting customer loyalty. Quality products not only drive sales but also enhance brand reputation and create a strong foundation for long-term success.

Innovation and Adaptability

Estee Lauder's ability to innovate and adapt to changing market trends was another key factor in her success. She was always looking for new ways to meet the needs of her customers and stay ahead of the competition. Estee's willingness to take risks and experiment with new ideas helped her to create groundbreaking products and marketing strategies that set her brand apart.

One example of Estee Lauder's innovative spirit is the introduction of Youth-Dew in 1953. At a time when women primarily used perfume for special occasions, Estee saw an opportunity to create a product that could be used daily. Youth-Dew was a bath oil that doubled as a perfume, offering a luxurious and affordable fragrance option for women. The success of Youth-Dew demonstrated Estee's ability to anticipate market trends and create products that resonated with consumers.

Estee Lauder's adaptability was also evident in her approach to international expansion. She recognized the potential for growth in international markets and was quick to tailor her products and marketing campaigns to meet the cultural preferences of different regions. This ability to adapt to diverse markets helped Estee Lauder Companies to become a global leader in the beauty industry.

In today's fast-paced business environment, innovation and adaptability are essential for success. Entrepreneurs can learn from Estee Lauder's example by staying attuned to market trends, being open to new ideas, and being willing to take calculated risks. Innovation is not just about creating new products; it is about finding new ways to meet the needs of customers and deliver value.

Building a Strong Brand Identity

Estee Lauder's success was built on a strong brand identity that communicated elegance, luxury, and quality. She understood that a brand is more than just a logo or a product; it is an experience and a promise to customers. Estee Lauder's brand identity was carefully crafted to reflect her values and resonate with her target audience.

One of the ways Estee Lauder built a strong brand identity was through consistent messaging and imagery. Her advertising campaigns featured sophisticated and aspirational images that appealed to the desires and aspirations of her customers. The messaging emphasized the luxurious and high-quality nature of Estee Lauder products, reinforcing the brand's premium positioning.

Estee Lauder also invested in creating a cohesive and recognizable visual identity. The packaging of Estee Lauder products was elegant and distinctive, making them stand out on store shelves. The use of signature colors, fonts, and design elements helped to create a consistent and memorable brand image.

A strong brand identity is crucial for building customer loyalty and differentiating a brand in a competitive market. Entrepreneurs can learn from Estee Lauder's approach by investing in brand development and ensuring that their brand identity aligns with their values and resonates with their target audience. Consistency in branding and messaging helps to build trust and create a strong emotional connection with customers.

Customer-Centric Approach

Estee Lauder's customer-centric approach was a key driver of her success. She believed that understanding and meeting the needs of her customers was essential for building a successful brand. Estee's hands-on approach to customer service and her commitment to personalized experiences set her apart from competitors.

Estee Lauder's emphasis on customer feedback was an important aspect of her customer-centric approach. She actively sought feedback from customers and used it to improve her products and services. Estee's willingness to listen to her customers and make changes based on their input helped to build trust and loyalty.

In addition to gathering feedback, Estee Lauder invested in training her beauty advisors to provide personalized consultations and recommendations. This focus on personalized service created a positive and memorable experience for customers, reinforcing their loyalty to the brand. Estee Lauder's customer-centric approach demonstrated that putting customers first can drive business success.

In today's business environment, a customer-centric approach is more important than ever. Entrepreneurs can learn from Estee Lauder's example by actively seeking customer feedback, investing in personalized service, and continuously striving to meet the needs and expectations of their customers. A customer-centric approach not only drives sales but also builds strong and lasting relationships with customers. Estee Lauder's impact on the modern beauty industry is profound and enduring. Her innovative marketing strategies, commitment to quality, and customer-centric approach set new standards for the industry and continue to influence beauty brands worldwide. Estee Lauder's ability to build a strong personal brand, prioritize product quality, and adapt to changing market trends offers valuable lessons for entrepreneurs and business leaders.

By understanding and applying the principles that guided Estee Lauder's success, modern entrepreneurs can navigate the challenges of the business world and build strong, resilient brands. Estee Lauder's legacy is a testament to the power of vision, perseverance, and innovation. Her journey serves as an inspiration and a blueprint for those who aspire to make a lasting impact in their industries.

Chapter 3: Mary Kay Ash - The Direct Selling Pioneer

Mary Kay Ash, born Mary Kathlyn Wagner on May 12, 1918, in Hot Wells, Texas, was destined to become a trailblazer in the world of direct selling. Growing up during the Great Depression, Mary Kay witnessed firsthand the struggles and resilience required to navigate tough economic times. Her father, Edward Alexander Wagner, was severely ill, leaving her mother, Lula Vember Hastings Wagner, to support the family. This dynamic forced Mary Kay to mature quickly and shoulder significant responsibilities from a young age.

Mary Kay's mother worked long hours as a nurse, often leaving Mary Kay to manage household duties and care for her ailing father. Despite these challenges, her mother instilled in her a powerful message that would shape her future: "You can do it." This encouragement fueled Mary Kay's belief in her capabilities and her determination to succeed, regardless of the obstacles she faced.

After graduating from Reagan High School in Houston, Mary Kay attended college for a short time but soon left to marry Ben Rogers in 1935. The couple had three children: Richard, Ben Jr., and Marylyn. However, the marriage was not to last, and they divorced in 1945. As a single mother, Mary Kay needed to provide for her family, which led her to pursue a career in direct sales.

Mary Kay began her career selling books door-to-door and later worked for Stanley Home Products, a company known for its direct selling model. Her natural talent for sales quickly became evident, and she excelled in her role, earning numerous promotions. However, despite her successes, she frequently encountered gender discrimination and saw male colleagues promoted over her, even when she outperformed them.

In 1952, Mary Kay joined World Gifts, another direct selling company. She rapidly rose through the ranks, but once again, her progress was stymied by the company's preference for promoting men. Frustrated by the glass ceiling she repeatedly encountered, Mary Kay decided to take control of her destiny and create her own company where women could thrive based on their abilities.

Achievements: Founding Mary Kay Inc. and Creating a Successful Direct Selling Model

In 1963, with a $5,000 investment from her life savings and financial support from her son, Richard Rogers, Mary Kay Ash founded Beauty by Mary Kay, which later became Mary Kay Inc. The company was built on Mary Kay's vision of providing women with opportunities for financial independence, personal growth, and recognition. From the outset, Mary Kay's mission was to empower women, a revolutionary idea at a time when women's career opportunities were limited.

Mary Kay Inc. started with a single storefront in Dallas, Texas, and a handful of beauty products. Mary

Kay's business model was unique and innovative: it combined the direct selling approach with a focus on empowering women as independent beauty consultants. This model not only allowed women to earn income but also provided them with the flexibility to balance work and family responsibilities.

One of Mary Kay's key innovations was the development of the "party plan" sales method. This involved beauty consultants hosting parties where they could demonstrate products and offer personalized beauty advice in a social setting. The party plan created a fun, interactive experience that fostered a sense of community and camaraderie among women. It also proved to be an incredibly effective sales strategy, driving product sales and recruiting new consultants.

Mary Kay's emphasis on personal development and recognition was another cornerstone of her business model. She believed in the power of positive reinforcement and created a culture where consultants were celebrated for their achievements. The company's incentive programs, such as the iconic pink Cadillac, diamond jewelry, and luxury trips, became legendary and highly motivating for consultants.

Mary Kay's marketing strategies were also groundbreaking. She understood the importance of branding and created a consistent, recognizable image for her company. The use of the color pink in packaging, promotional materials, and even the Cadillacs awarded to top sellers became a distinctive trademark. This cohesive branding helped to differentiate Mary Kay Inc. from other beauty companies and established a strong brand identity.

Under Mary Kay's leadership, the company experienced rapid growth. By the end of its first year, Mary Kay Inc. had over 100 beauty consultants and $198,000 in sales. The company's success continued to soar, expanding across the United States and eventually internationally. Mary Kay Inc. entered the Canadian market in 1971, followed by Australia in 1975, and later expanded to Europe, Asia, and Latin America.

Mary Kay's commitment to empowering women extended beyond her company. She was an advocate for women's rights and equality, often speaking on these issues and participating in related organizations. In 1980, she established the Mary Kay Ash Charitable Foundation, which supports cancer research and efforts to end domestic violence. Her philanthropic efforts further solidified her legacy as a champion for women.

Mary Kay's achievements have had a lasting impact on the direct selling industry and women's entrepreneurship. By creating a company that valued and empowered women, she not only built a successful business but also inspired countless women to pursue their own entrepreneurial dreams. Her innovative business model, focus on personal development, and commitment to recognizing and rewarding achievement set new standards in the industry.

Impact on Industry: Shaping the Modern Direct Selling Industry

Mary Kay Ash's influence on the direct selling industry is profound and enduring. She revolutionized the way direct sales were conducted and demonstrated that empowering women could be both a socially responsible and highly effective business strategy.

Transforming Direct Sales with the Party Plan

One of Mary Kay's most significant contributions to the direct selling industry was the introduction of the party plan sales method. This approach transformed the traditional door-to-door sales model by creating a social and interactive environment for product demonstrations and sales. Beauty consultants would host parties in their homes or the homes of friends, inviting guests to try products, receive personalized beauty advice, and enjoy a fun, social gathering.

The party plan was a game-changer for several reasons. First, it provided a comfortable and relaxed setting for customers, making them more receptive to trying new products and making purchases. The social aspect of the parties also encouraged word-of-mouth marketing, as guests who enjoyed the experience would share it with their friends and family.

Second, the party plan fostered a sense of community among women. It created opportunities for women to connect, share experiences, and support each other. This sense of community was particularly empowering for women who were often isolated due to family responsibilities or limited career opportunities.

Finally, the party plan was an effective recruitment tool. Guests who attended parties and saw the success of the beauty consultant often expressed interest in becoming consultants themselves. This approach allowed Mary Kay Inc. to grow its network of consultants organically and rapidly, creating a scalable and sustainable business model.

Empowering Women through Entrepreneurship

Mary Kay Ash's vision of empowering women was at the heart of her business model. She believed that women should have the opportunity to achieve financial independence and personal fulfillment through entrepreneurship. By creating a flexible and supportive environment, Mary Kay Inc. enabled women to build successful businesses on their own terms.

The company's emphasis on personal development and recognition was instrumental in fostering a positive and motivating culture. Mary Kay believed that every person had potential and that it was the company's responsibility to help them realize it. This philosophy was reflected in the extensive training and support provided to beauty consultants, as well as the numerous recognition and incentive programs.

The iconic pink Cadillac became a symbol of success and achievement within Mary Kay Inc. Introduced in 1969, the pink Cadillac was awarded to top-performing beauty consultants as a tangible reward for their hard work and dedication. This incentive program not only motivated consultants to strive for excellence but also created a powerful symbol of empowerment and success.

Mary Kay's approach to recognition and incentives went beyond material rewards. The company celebrated achievements through annual events such as the Seminar, where consultants were recognized for their accomplishments, received training, and participated in motivational sessions. These events reinforced the company's commitment to personal development and created a sense of pride and belonging among consultants.

Establishing a Strong Brand Identity

Mary Kay Ash understood the importance of branding and created a strong, cohesive brand identity for her company. The use of the color pink became a signature element of the Mary Kay brand, symbolizing femininity, elegance, and empowerment. Pink was incorporated into product packaging, promotional materials, and even the Cadillacs awarded to top consultants.

The consistent use of pink helped to create a recognizable and memorable brand image. Customers and consultants alike associated the color with Mary Kay Inc. and its values. This strong brand identity differentiated Mary Kay from competitors and contributed to the company's enduring success.

In addition to the visual elements of the brand, Mary

Kay's personal brand played a crucial role in shaping the company's image. Mary Kay herself became a symbol of the company's values and mission. Her charisma, warmth, and dedication to empowering women were central to the brand's identity. Mary Kay's presence in advertisements, training materials, and company events reinforced the personal connection between her and the consultants, creating a sense of trust and loyalty.

Pioneering Corporate Social Responsibility

Mary Kay Ash was ahead of her time in recognizing the importance of corporate social responsibility (CSR). She believed that businesses had a duty to give back to society and support important causes. This commitment to CSR was reflected in the company's philanthropic efforts and ethical business practices.

In 1980, Mary Kay Ash established the Mary Kay Ash Charitable Foundation, which focuses on funding cancer research and supporting efforts to end domestic violence. The foundation's work has had a significant impact, providing financial support to organizations and initiatives that address these critical issues. Mary Kay Inc.'s commitment to CSR has also enhanced the company's reputation and strengthened its connection with customers and consultants who value social responsibility.

Mary Kay's focus on ethical business practices extended to the company's approach to product development and sourcing. The company has long prioritized the safety and efficacy of its products, conducting rigorous testing to ensure they meet high standards. Mary Kay Inc. has also made efforts to source ingredients ethically and sustainably, reflecting a commitment to environmental responsibility.

The company's philanthropic and ethical initiatives have set a benchmark for other businesses in the beauty industry. By demonstrating that a company can be both profitable and socially responsible, Mary Kay Ash has inspired other brands to adopt similar practices and prioritize CSR.

Lessons Learned: The Importance of Personal Branding and Product Quality

Mary Kay Ash's journey offers invaluable lessons for aspiring entrepreneurs and business leaders. Her emphasis on personal branding and product quality were key factors in her success and continue to be relevant in today's business landscape.
The Power of Personal Branding

Mary Kay Ash's success can be attributed in large part to her mastery of personal branding. She understood that a strong personal brand could create a powerful connection with consumers and differentiate her products in a crowded market. Mary Kay's personal brand was synonymous with empowerment, elegance, and quality, and she leveraged this image to build a loyal customer base and establish her company as a leader in the beauty industry.

One of the key elements of Mary Kay's personal branding strategy was her hands-on approach. She was actively involved in every aspect of her business, from product development to marketing and sales.

Mary Kay's personal touch and attention to detail ensured that her products met the highest standards and reflected her values. This level of involvement also helped to build trust and credibility with customers, who appreciated her commitment to quality and excellence.

Mary Kay's personal brand was also characterized by her warmth and charisma. She cultivated a supportive and motivating environment within her company, creating a sense of community and belonging among consultants. Mary Kay's ability to connect with people on a personal level was a significant factor in the company's success.

In today's business world, personal branding remains a critical component of success. Entrepreneurs and business leaders can learn from Mary Kay's example by building strong, authentic personal brands that resonate with their target audience. Personal branding is not just about self-promotion; it is about conveying your values, vision, and unique qualities in a way that connects with others and builds trust.

The Importance of Product Quality

Another fundamental lesson from Mary Kay Ash's journey is the importance of product quality. Mary Kay was unwavering in her commitment to creating high-quality products that delivered on their promises. She believed that the best marketing in the world could not compensate for a subpar product, and she made quality the cornerstone of her brand.

Mary Kay's dedication to quality was evident in every

aspect of her products, from formulation to packaging. She worked closely with chemists and product developers to ensure that her skincare and makeup products met the highest standards of efficacy and safety. Mary Kay also paid meticulous attention to packaging, understanding that the presentation of a product could enhance its perceived value and appeal.

This focus on quality helped to differentiate Mary Kay products in a competitive market. Customers knew that when they purchased a Mary Kay product, they were getting something that was carefully crafted and rigorously tested. This reputation for quality built trust and loyalty, driving repeat purchases and word-of-mouth recommendations.

In addition to product quality, Mary Kay understood the importance of continuous innovation. She was constantly looking for ways to improve her products and introduce new offerings that met the evolving needs of her customers. This commitment to innovation ensured that Mary Kay stayed at the forefront of the beauty industry and maintained its competitive edge.

For modern entrepreneurs, the lesson is clear: product quality should never be compromised. Investing in high-quality ingredients, rigorous testing, and thoughtful design can set a brand apart and build lasting customer loyalty. Quality products not only drive sales but also enhance brand reputation and create a strong foundation for long-term success.

Building a Strong Brand Identity

Mary Kay Ash's success was built on a strong brand identity that communicated empowerment, elegance, and quality. She understood that a brand is more than just a logo or a product; it is an experience and a promise to customers. Mary Kay's brand identity was carefully crafted to reflect her values and resonate with her target audience.

One of the ways Mary Kay built a strong brand identity was through consistent messaging and imagery. Her advertising campaigns featured sophisticated and aspirational images that appealed to the desires and aspirations of her customers. The messaging emphasized the empowering and high-quality nature of Mary Kay products, reinforcing the brand's premium positioning.

Mary Kay also invested in creating a cohesive and recognizable visual identity. The use of the color pink in product packaging, promotional materials, and even the Cadillacs awarded to top consultants became a distinctive trademark. This consistent use of pink helped to create a recognizable and memorable brand image.

A strong brand identity is crucial for building customer loyalty and differentiating a brand in a competitive market. Entrepreneurs can learn from Mary Kay's approach by investing in brand development and ensuring that their brand identity aligns with their values and resonates with their target audience. Consistency in branding and messaging helps to build trust and create a strong emotional connection with customers.

Empowerment and Recognition

Mary Kay Ash's focus on empowerment and recognition was a key driver of her company's success. She believed that recognizing and celebrating achievements was essential for motivating and retaining talent. This philosophy was reflected in the numerous recognition and incentive programs at Mary Kay Inc.

The iconic pink Cadillac became a symbol of success and achievement within Mary Kay Inc. Introduced in 1969, the pink Cadillac was awarded to top-performing beauty consultants as a tangible reward for their hard work and dedication. This incentive program not only motivated consultants to strive for excellence but also created a powerful symbol of empowerment and success.

Mary Kay's approach to recognition went beyond material rewards. The company celebrated achievements through annual events such as the Seminar, where consultants were recognized for their accomplishments, received training, and participated in motivational sessions. These events reinforced the company's commitment to personal development and created a sense of pride and belonging among consultants.

In today's business environment, recognizing and celebrating achievements is more important than ever. Entrepreneurs can learn from Mary Kay's example by creating a culture of recognition and empowerment within their organizations. Recognizing and celebrating achievements not only motivates employees but also fosters a positive and supportive work environment.

Mary Kay Ash's remarkable journey and achievements have had a lasting impact on the direct selling industry and women's entrepreneurship. Her innovative business model, focus on personal development and recognition, and commitment to empowering women set new standards in the industry. Mary Kay's emphasis on personal branding, product quality, and customer-centricity offers valuable lessons for modern entrepreneurs and business leaders.

By understanding and applying the principles that guided Mary Kay Ash's success, aspiring entrepreneurs can navigate the challenges of the business world and build strong, resilient brands. Mary Kay Ash's legacy is a testament to the power of vision, perseverance, and innovation. Her journey serves as an inspiration and a blueprint for those who aspire to make a lasting impact in their industries.

Impact on Industry: Revolutionizing Direct Sales and Women's Entrepreneurship

Mary Kay Ash revolutionized the direct sales industry with her innovative strategies and a focus on empowering women. Her approach to direct sales was transformative, creating a new business model that emphasized personal development, community building, and entrepreneurial opportunities for women.

The Party Plan: A New Sales Model

One of Mary Kay's most significant contributions to the direct sales industry was the introduction of the party plan sales model. This approach transformed the traditional door-to-door sales method into a social and interactive experience. Beauty consultants would host parties in their homes or the homes of friends, inviting guests to try products, receive personalized beauty advice, and enjoy a fun, social gathering.

The party plan was revolutionary for several reasons. Firstly, it provided a comfortable and relaxed setting for customers, making them more receptive to trying new products and making purchases. The social aspect of the parties also encouraged word-of-mouth marketing, as guests who enjoyed the experience would share it with their friends and family.

Secondly, the party plan fostered a sense of community among women. It created opportunities for women to connect, share experiences, and support each other. This sense of community was particularly empowering for women who were often isolated due to family responsibilities or limited career opportunities.

Finally, the party plan was an effective recruitment tool. Guests who attended parties and saw the success of the beauty consultant often expressed interest in becoming consultants themselves. This approach allowed Mary Kay Inc. to grow its network of consultants organically and rapidly, creating a scalable and sustainable business model.

Empowering Women through Entrepreneurship

Mary Kay Ash's vision of empowering women was at the heart of her business model. She believed that women should have the opportunity to achieve financial independence and personal fulfillment through entrepreneurship. By creating a flexible and supportive environment, Mary Kay Inc. enabled women to build successful businesses on their own terms.

The company's emphasis on personal development and recognition was instrumental in fostering a positive and motivating culture. Mary Kay believed that every person had potential and that it was the company's responsibility to help them realize it. This philosophy was reflected in the extensive training and support provided to beauty consultants, as well as the numerous recognition and incentive programs.

The iconic pink Cadillac became a symbol of success and achievement within Mary Kay Inc. Introduced in 1969, the pink Cadillac was awarded to top-performing beauty consultants as a tangible reward for their hard work and dedication. This incentive program not only motivated consultants to strive for excellence but also created a powerful symbol of empowerment and success.

Mary Kay's marketing strategies were also groundbreaking. She understood the importance of branding and created a consistent, recognizable image for her company. The use of the color pink in packaging, promotional materials, and even the Cadillacs awarded to top sellers became a distinctive trademark. This cohesive branding helped to differentiate Mary Kay Inc. from other beauty companies and established a strong brand identity.

Under Mary Kay's leadership, the company experienced rapid growth. By the end of its first year, Mary Kay Inc. had over 100 beauty consultants and $198,000 in sales. The company's success continued to soar, expanding across the United States and eventually internationally. Mary Kay Inc. entered the Canadian market in 1971, followed by Australia in 1975, and later expanded to Europe, Asia, and Latin America.

Mary Kay's commitment to empowering women extended beyond her company. She was an advocate for women's rights and equality, often speaking on these issues and participating in related organizations. In 1980, she established the Mary Kay Ash Charitable Foundation, which supports cancer research and efforts to end domestic violence. Her philanthropic efforts further solidified her legacy as a champion for women.

Mary Kay's achievements have had a lasting impact on the direct selling industry and women's entrepreneurship. By creating a company that valued and empowered women, she not only built a successful business but also inspired countless women to pursue their own entrepreneurial dreams. Her innovative business model, focus on personal development, and commitment to recognizing and rewarding achievement set new standards in the industry.

Global Expansion and Influence

Mary Kay Ash's impact on the direct selling industry extended far beyond the United States. She recognized the potential for international growth early on and pursued an aggressive global expansion strategy. By the 1970s, Mary Kay products were available in major cities around the world, from London and Paris to Tokyo and Hong Kong.

Mary Kay's approach to international expansion was strategic and thoughtful. She ensured that her products and marketing campaigns were tailored to the cultural and aesthetic preferences of each market. This localization strategy helped to establish the Mary Kay brand as a global leader in beauty, respected and loved by consumers worldwide.

Today, Mary Kay Inc. operates in over 40 countries, with a diverse portfolio of brands that cater to a global audience. The company's success in international markets is a testament to Mary Kay's vision and strategic foresight. Her ability to build a global brand without compromising on quality or customer experience set a new standard for international business expansion in the beauty industry.

Pioneering Corporate Social Responsibility

Mary Kay Ash was ahead of her time in recognizing the importance of corporate social responsibility (CSR). She believed that businesses had a duty to give back to society and support important causes. This commitment to CSR was reflected in the company's philanthropic efforts and ethical business practices.

In 1980, Mary Kay Ash established the Mary Kay Ash Charitable Foundation, which focuses on funding cancer research and supporting efforts to end domestic violence. The foundation's work has had a significant impact, providing financial support to organizations and initiatives that address these critical issues. Mary Kay Inc.'s commitment to CSR has also enhanced the company's reputation and strengthened its connection with customers and consultants who value social responsibility.

Mary Kay's focus on ethical business practices extended to the company's approach to product development and sourcing. The company has long prioritized the safety and efficacy of its products, conducting rigorous testing to ensure they meet high standards. Mary Kay Inc. has also made efforts to source ingredients ethically and sustainably, reflecting a commitment to environmental responsibility.

The company's philanthropic and ethical initiatives have set a benchmark for other businesses in the beauty industry. By demonstrating that a company can be both profitable and socially responsible, Mary Kay Ash has inspired other brands to adopt similar practices and prioritize CSR.

Impact on Women's Entrepreneurship

Mary Kay Ash's influence on women's entrepreneurship is profound and enduring. Her vision of empowering women through entrepreneurship has inspired countless women to start their own businesses and pursue their dreams. Mary Kay Inc.'s success has demonstrated that women can excel in business and achieve financial independence and personal fulfillment.

Mary Kay's emphasis on personal development and recognition has also had a lasting impact on women's entrepreneurship. By creating a supportive and motivating environment, Mary Kay Inc. has helped women to realize their potential and achieve their goals. The company's recognition and incentive programs have set new standards for employee motivation and retention, inspiring other businesses to adopt similar practices.

Mary Kay Ash's legacy as a pioneer of women's entrepreneurship is a testament to her vision, determination, and commitment to empowering women. Her innovative business model, focus on personal development, and commitment to recognizing and rewarding achievement have set new standards in the industry and continue to inspire future generations of women entrepreneurs.

Lessons Learned: Empowering Others and Building a Strong Network

Mary Kay Ash's success was built on a foundation of empowerment. She believed that every person had the potential to achieve great things, and it was her mission to help them realize that potential. This philosophy was reflected in the extensive training and support provided to beauty consultants, as well as the numerous recognition and incentive programs.

Mary Kay's emphasis on empowerment was not just about financial success; it was about personal growth and fulfillment. She believed that by empowering others, she could create a positive and motivating environment where people could thrive. This focus on personal development and empowerment was instrumental in fostering a positive and motivating culture at Mary Kay Inc.

One of the key elements of Mary Kay's empowerment strategy was her focus on positive reinforcement. She believed that recognizing and celebrating achievements was essential for motivating and retaining talent. The company's recognition and incentive programs, such as the iconic pink Cadillac, were designed to celebrate success and inspire consultants to strive for excellence.

Mary Kay's approach to empowerment also extended to her leadership style. She believed in leading by example and was actively involved in every aspect of her business. Her hands-on approach and genuine interest in her consultants' success created a strong sense of trust and loyalty. Mary Kay's ability to connect with people on a personal level was a significant factor in the company's success.

In today's business environment, empowerment is more important than ever. Entrepreneurs and business leaders can learn from Mary Kay's example by creating a culture of empowerment within their organizations. Empowering others not only drives business success but also fosters a positive and supportive work environment.

Building a Strong Network

Another fundamental lesson from Mary Kay Ash's journey is the importance of building a strong network. Mary Kay understood that success was not achieved in isolation; it required the support and collaboration of others. She believed in the power of community and created a supportive and motivating environment where women could connect, share experiences, and support each other.

The company's emphasis on personal development and recognition was instrumental in fostering a positive and motivating culture. Mary Kay believed that every person had potential and that it was the company's responsibility to help them realize it. This philosophy was reflected in the extensive training and support provided to beauty consultants, as well as the numerous recognition and incentive programs.

The iconic pink Cadillac became a symbol of success and achievement within Mary Kay Inc. Introduced in 1969, the pink Cadillac was awarded to top-performing beauty consultants as a tangible reward for their hard work and dedication. This incentive program not only motivated consultants to strive for excellence but also created a powerful symbol of empowerment and success.

Mary Kay's marketing strategies were also groundbreaking. She understood the importance of branding and created a consistent, recognizable image for her company. The use of the color pink in packaging, promotional materials, and even the

Cadillacs awarded to top sellers became a distinctive trademark. This cohesive branding helped to differentiate Mary Kay Inc. from other beauty companies and established a strong brand identity.

Under Mary Kay's leadership, the company experienced rapid growth. By the end of its first year, Mary Kay Inc. had over 100 beauty consultants and $198,000 in sales. The company's success continued to soar, expanding across the United States and eventually internationally. Mary Kay Inc. entered the Canadian market in 1971, followed by Australia in 1975, and later expanded to Europe, Asia, and Latin America.

Mary Kay's commitment to empowering women extended beyond her company. She was an advocate for women's rights and equality, often speaking on these issues and participating in related organizations. In 1980, she established the Mary Kay Ash Charitable Foundation, which supports cancer research and efforts to end domestic violence. Her philanthropic efforts further solidified her legacy as a champion for women.

Mary Kay's achievements have had a lasting impact on the direct selling industry and women's entrepreneurship. By creating a company that valued and empowered women, she not only built a successful business but also inspired countless women to pursue their own entrepreneurial dreams. Her innovative business model, focus on personal development, and commitment to recognizing and rewarding achievement set new standards in the industry.

Networking for Success

Mary Kay Ash understood that building a strong network was essential for success in business. She believed that by connecting with others and building relationships, she could create opportunities for growth and collaboration. This focus on networking was a key factor in the success of Mary Kay Inc.

One of the ways Mary Kay built a strong network was through the company's extensive training and support programs. These programs provided beauty consultants with the knowledge and skills they needed to succeed, as well as opportunities to connect with other consultants and share experiences. This sense of community and support was instrumental in fostering a positive and motivating culture at Mary Kay Inc.

Mary Kay also believed in the power of mentorship. She recognized that experienced consultants could provide valuable guidance and support to new recruits, helping them to navigate the challenges of building a business. The company's mentorship programs created opportunities for consultants to learn from each other and build strong, supportive relationships.

In addition to internal networking, Mary Kay understood the importance of building relationships with external partners. She established strong partnerships with suppliers, retailers, and other stakeholders, creating a network of support that contributed to the company's success. These relationships were built on trust and mutual benefit, reflecting Mary Kay's commitment to ethical business practices and collaboration.

In today's business environment, networking is more important than ever. Entrepreneurs and business leaders can learn from Mary Kay's example by building strong networks within their organizations and with external partners. Networking not only creates opportunities for growth and collaboration but also provides valuable support and resources for navigating the challenges of entrepreneurship.

Leadership and Mentorship

Mary Kay Ash's leadership style was characterized by her focus on empowerment and mentorship. She believed that a successful leader should inspire and support others, helping them to realize their potential and achieve their goals. This philosophy was reflected in the company's leadership and mentorship programs, which provided beauty consultants with the guidance and support they needed to succeed.

Mary Kay's approach to leadership was hands-on and personal. She was actively involved in every aspect of her business, from product development to marketing and sales. Her genuine interest in her consultants' success created a strong sense of trust and loyalty, and her ability to connect with people on a personal level was a significant factor in the company's success.

One of the key elements of Mary Kay's leadership strategy was her focus on positive reinforcement. She believed that recognizing and celebrating achievements was essential for motivating and retaining talent. The company's recognition and incentive programs, such as the iconic pink Cadillac, were designed to celebrate success and inspire consultants to strive for excellence.

Mary Kay's mentorship programs created opportunities for experienced consultants to provide guidance and support to new recruits. These programs not only helped new consultants to navigate the challenges of building a business but also fostered a sense of community and collaboration within the company. The mentorship programs were instrumental in creating a positive and motivating culture at Mary Kay Inc.

In today's business environment, effective leadership and mentorship are more important than ever. Entrepreneurs and business leaders can learn from Mary Kay's example by creating a culture of empowerment and mentorship within their organizations. Empowering others and providing mentorship not only drives business success but also fosters a positive and supportive work environment.

Mary Kay Ash's remarkable journey and achievements have had a lasting impact on the direct selling industry and women's entrepreneurship. Her innovative business model, focus on personal development and recognition, and commitment to empowering women set new standards in the industry. Mary Kay's emphasis on personal branding, product quality, and customer-centricity offers valuable lessons for modern entrepreneurs and business leaders.

By understanding and applying the principles that

guided Mary Kay Ash's success, aspiring entrepreneurs can navigate the challenges of the business world and build strong, resilient brands. Mary Kay Ash's legacy is a testament to the power of vision, perseverance, and innovation. Her journey serves as an inspiration and a blueprint for those who aspire to make a lasting impact in their industries.

Chapter 4: Oprah Winfrey - The Media Powerhouse

Oprah Winfrey's story is one of resilience, determination, and extraordinary success. Born on January 29, 1954, in Kosciusko, Mississippi, Oprah Gail Winfrey faced significant challenges from the outset. Raised by her grandmother in abject poverty, Oprah's early life was marked by hardship. Her grandmother, Hattie Mae Lee, taught her to read at an early age, instilling in her a love of books and a passion for learning.

Despite these early influences, Oprah's childhood was tumultuous. At the age of six, she moved to Milwaukee, Wisconsin, to live with her mother, Vernita Lee. The environment was far from stable; Oprah experienced severe abuse and neglect during these years. She was moved to live with her father, Vernon Winfrey, in Nashville, Tennessee, during her early teens, where she found more stability and support.

Vernon Winfrey was a strict but loving figure who emphasized the importance of education and discipline. Under his guidance, Oprah flourished academically and socially. She excelled in school, becoming an honors student and earning a full scholarship to Tennessee State University, where she majored in speech communication and performing arts.

Oprah's entry into media began unexpectedly. At 17,

she won a beauty pageant, which led to a part-time job at a local black radio station, WVOL, in Nashville. Her natural talent for communication and her charismatic personality quickly became apparent, and she was soon offered a job as a news anchor at a local television station. Oprah became the first African American female news anchor at Nashville's WLAC-TV.

Her career continued to ascend as she moved to Baltimore, Maryland, in 1976 to co-anchor the evening news at WJZ-TV. However, it was her role as a co-host on the talk show "People Are Talking" that truly allowed her to shine. Her empathetic interviewing style and ability to connect with both guests and the audience set her apart. Oprah's success on "People Are Talking" led to an offer to host her own morning show, "A.M. Chicago," in 1984.

Oprah's relocation to Chicago marked a turning point in her career. She transformed "A.M. Chicago" from a low-rated local talk show into a highly successful program. Within months, the show was renamed "The Oprah Winfrey Show." Oprah's authentic, engaging style resonated with viewers, and the show rapidly gained national syndication in 1986. "The Oprah Winfrey Show" became a cultural phenomenon, eventually airing in 144 countries and reaching millions of viewers.

Achievements: Creating Harpo Productions and the Oprah Winfrey Network

Oprah's success with "The Oprah Winfrey Show" provided the foundation for her to expand her influence and create her own media empire. In 1986, she founded Harpo Productions, a multimedia production company. The name "Harpo" is "Oprah" spelled backward, symbolizing her forward-thinking vision and the reversal of traditional media power dynamics.

Harpo Productions: Building a Media Empire

Harpo Productions was groundbreaking in several ways. As one of the first African American women to own a production company, Oprah broke barriers in an industry dominated by white men. Harpo Productions gave Oprah full control over her brand and content, allowing her to produce high-quality, impactful programming that reflected her values and vision.

Harpo Productions quickly expanded its portfolio, producing a wide range of television programs, films, and publications. One of its most successful ventures was the production of "The Oprah Winfrey Show," which ran for 25 years and became the highest-rated talk show in American television history. The show's success was due in large part to Oprah's unique approach to storytelling and her ability to address a wide range of topics, from personal development and health to social issues and celebrity interviews.

In addition to "The Oprah Winfrey Show," Harpo Productions produced several other successful television programs, including "Dr. Phil," "Rachael Ray," and "The Dr. Oz Show." These spin-offs further solidified Harpo Productions' reputation as a powerhouse in daytime television. Oprah's ability to identify and nurture talent was a key factor in the success of these shows.

Harpo Productions also ventured into film production, with notable projects including the critically acclaimed film "The Color Purple" (1985), in which Oprah made her acting debut. The film, produced by Steven Spielberg and based on Alice Walker's Pulitzer Prize-winning novel, received 11 Academy Award nominations. Oprah's performance as Sofia earned her an Academy Award nomination for Best Supporting Actress, showcasing her talent and versatility as an entertainer.

The Oprah Winfrey Network: A New Era of Influence

Oprah's media empire continued to grow with the launch of the Oprah Winfrey Network (OWN) in January 2011. OWN was a joint venture with Discovery Communications, aimed at creating a network that reflected Oprah's commitment to inspiring and empowering content. The network's mission was to offer programming that uplifted and enlightened viewers, promoting personal growth, health, and well-being.

OWN's programming includes a mix of talk shows, documentaries, reality TV, and original scripted series. Some of the network's most popular shows include "Super Soul Sunday," "Oprah's Master Class," and "Iyanla: Fix My Life." These programs embody Oprah's vision of providing meaningful and transformative content.

"Super Soul Sunday" features interviews with thought leaders, authors, and spiritual teachers, exploring topics related to spirituality, mindfulness, and personal development. "Oprah's Master Class" offers an intimate look at the lives and careers of successful individuals, sharing their life lessons and insights. "Iyanla: Fix My Life," hosted by life coach Iyanla Vanzant, helps individuals and families overcome personal challenges and improve their lives.

OWN's original scripted series have also garnered critical acclaim and a dedicated audience. Shows like "Queen Sugar," created by Ava DuVernay and executive produced by Oprah, and "Greenleaf," executive produced by Oprah and Craig Wright, have received praise for their storytelling, diversity, and social relevance. These series have contributed to the network's success and reinforced Oprah's commitment to promoting diverse voices and stories.

In addition to its programming, OWN has also launched initiatives to support social causes and community engagement. The network's "OWN Your Life" campaign encourages viewers to take control of their lives and make positive changes, while the "OWN Ambassadors" program recognizes individuals who are making a difference in their communities.

OWN's success is a testament to Oprah's vision and leadership. Despite initial challenges and lower-than-expected ratings, Oprah's unwavering commitment to her mission and her ability to adapt and innovate have made OWN a respected and influential network. The network's focus on meaningful and transformative content has resonated with viewers, creating a loyal audience and a strong brand.

Impact on Media and Culture

Oprah Winfrey's influence extends far beyond her own media ventures. She has had a profound impact on the media industry and popular culture, changing the way stories are told and the types of stories that are given a platform. Oprah's commitment to authenticity, empathy, and empowerment has set a new standard for media and entertainment.

One of Oprah's most significant contributions is her ability to create a space for important social issues and conversations. Throughout her career, she has used her platform to address topics such as race, gender, mental health, and personal development. By sharing her own experiences and inviting diverse voices to share theirs, Oprah has helped to destigmatize these issues and promote greater understanding and empathy.

Oprah's book club, launched in 1996, is another example of her impact on culture. The Oprah's Book Club has introduced millions of readers to a wide range of authors and genres, promoting a love of reading and supporting the literary community. Many of the books selected for the club have become bestsellers, and the club has played a significant role in shaping literary trends and discussions.

In addition to her work in media, Oprah's philanthropic efforts have had a significant impact on education, health, and social justice. The Oprah Winfrey Foundation and the Oprah Winfrey

Operating Foundation support a variety of causes, including scholarships for students, funding for schools and educational programs, and support for organizations working to improve health and well-being.

One of Oprah's most notable philanthropic projects is the Oprah Winfrey Leadership Academy for Girls in South Africa. Founded in 2007, the academy provides education and leadership training to girls from disadvantaged backgrounds, empowering them to become leaders in their communities and beyond. The academy reflects Oprah's belief in the transformative power of education and her commitment to creating opportunities for young women.

Legacy and Influence

Oprah Winfrey's legacy is one of empowerment, authenticity, and transformative influence. Her journey from poverty to media mogul is a testament to her resilience, determination, and vision. Oprah's ability to connect with people on a deep and personal level has made her a beloved figure and a powerful force for positive change.

Oprah's influence can be seen in the countless lives she has touched through her media ventures, philanthropic efforts, and personal interactions. Her commitment to empowering others and promoting meaningful content has set a new standard for media and entertainment. Oprah's legacy continues to inspire and motivate individuals around the world to pursue their dreams and make a difference.

Oprah Winfrey's remarkable journey and achievements have had a lasting impact on the media industry and popular culture. Her innovative approach to storytelling, her commitment to empowering others, and her dedication to meaningful and transformative content have set new standards and inspired countless individuals. Oprah's legacy is a testament to the power of vision, resilience, and authenticity. Her journey serves as an inspiration and a blueprint for those who aspire to make a lasting impact in their industries and the world.

Oprah's story is one of triumph over adversity, demonstrating that with determination, hard work, and a clear vision, it is possible to achieve extraordinary success and make a significant impact. Her journey from poverty to media mogul is a powerful reminder that our circumstances do not define us; our choices and actions do. Oprah's ability to transform her life and the lives of others is a testament to her incredible spirit and unwavering commitment to making a difference.

Lessons Learned: Empowering Others and Building a Strong Network

Oprah Winfrey's journey offers invaluable lessons for aspiring entrepreneurs and business leaders. Her emphasis on empowering others and building a strong network were key factors in her success and continue to be relevant in today's business landscape.

Empowering Others

One of the fundamental lessons from Oprah Winfrey's

journey is the importance of empowering others. Throughout her career, Oprah has used her platform to uplift and inspire individuals, providing them with the tools and resources they need to succeed. Her commitment to empowerment is evident in her media ventures, philanthropic efforts, and personal interactions.

Oprah's approach to empowerment is multifaceted. She believes in the power of storytelling and uses her platform to share stories that inspire and educate. By highlighting the experiences and achievements of others, Oprah has created a space for diverse voices and perspectives, promoting greater understanding and empathy.

In addition to storytelling, Oprah emphasizes the importance of education and personal development. Through initiatives such as the Oprah Winfrey Leadership Academy for Girls and the Oprah's Book Club, she has provided individuals with opportunities to learn, grow, and achieve their goals. Oprah's commitment to education reflects her belief in its transformative power and its ability to create lasting change.

Oprah's leadership style is also characterized by her focus on empowerment. She leads by example, demonstrating the importance of authenticity, empathy, and resilience. Oprah's ability to connect with people on a personal level and inspire them to reach their full potential has been a significant factor in her success.

In today's business environment, empowerment is

more important than ever. Entrepreneurs and business leaders can learn from Oprah's example by creating a culture of empowerment within their organizations. Empowering others not only drives business success but also fosters a positive and supportive work environment.

Building a Strong Network

Another fundamental lesson from Oprah Winfrey's journey is the importance of building a strong network. Oprah understood that success was not achieved in isolation; it required the support and collaboration of others. She believed in the power of community and created a supportive and motivating environment where individuals could connect, share experiences, and support each other.

One of the ways Oprah built a strong network was through her extensive media ventures. By creating platforms such as "The Oprah Winfrey Show" and the Oprah Winfrey Network, she provided individuals with opportunities to share their stories and connect with a broader audience. These platforms created a sense of community and support, fostering a positive and motivating environment.

Oprah also believed in the power of mentorship. She recognized that experienced individuals could provide valuable guidance and support to those just starting their journeys. Throughout her career, Oprah has mentored and supported numerous individuals, helping them to navigate the challenges of the media industry and achieve their goals.

In addition to internal networking, Oprah understood the importance of building relationships with external partners. She established strong partnerships with other media companies, production studios, and organizations, creating a network of support that contributed to her success. These relationships were built on trust and mutual benefit, reflecting Oprah's commitment to ethical business practices and collaboration.

In today's business environment, networking is more important than ever. Entrepreneurs and business leaders can learn from Oprah's example by building strong networks within their organizations and with external partners. Networking not only creates opportunities for growth and collaboration but also provides valuable support and resources for navigating the challenges of entrepreneurship.

Authenticity and Empathy

Oprah Winfrey's success is also a testament to the power of authenticity and empathy. Throughout her career, Oprah has remained true to herself and her values, creating a brand that is synonymous with trust and integrity. Her ability to connect with people on a deep and personal level has been a significant factor in her success.

Oprah's authenticity is evident in her approach to storytelling. She shares her own experiences and vulnerabilities, creating a space for others to do the same. By being open and honest about her own challenges and triumphs, Oprah has built a strong emotional connection with her audience, fostering trust and loyalty.

Empathy is another key element of Oprah's success. Her ability to understand and relate to the experiences of others has made her a powerful and influential figure. Oprah's empathetic approach to interviewing and storytelling has created a space for important conversations and promoted greater understanding and compassion.

In today's business environment, authenticity and empathy are more important than ever. Entrepreneurs and business leaders can learn from Oprah's example by creating a culture of authenticity and empathy within their organizations. These qualities not only build trust and loyalty but also foster a positive and supportive work environment.

Innovation and Adaptability

Oprah Winfrey's journey is also a testament to the power of innovation and adaptability. Throughout her career, Oprah has demonstrated an ability to anticipate and respond to changes in the media industry, positioning herself as a leader and innovator.

One of the key elements of Oprah's success is her willingness to take risks and explore new opportunities. From launching Harpo Productions to creating the Oprah Winfrey Network, Oprah has consistently pushed the boundaries of traditional media and created new and innovative platforms. Her ability to identify and capitalize on emerging trends has been a significant factor in her success.

Oprah's adaptability is also evident in her approach to content creation. She has consistently evolved her programming to reflect the changing needs and interests of her audience, from the talk show format of "The Oprah Winfrey Show" to the diverse and dynamic programming of the Oprah Winfrey Network. Oprah's ability to adapt and innovate has ensured her continued relevance and influence in the media industry.

In today's fast-paced business environment, innovation and adaptability are essential for success. Entrepreneurs and business leaders can learn from Oprah's example by staying attuned to market trends, being open to new ideas, and being willing to take calculated risks. Innovation is not just about creating new products or services; it is about finding new ways to meet the needs of customers and deliver value.

Oprah Winfrey's remarkable journey from poverty to media mogul is a testament to her resilience, determination, and vision. Her innovative approach to storytelling, commitment to empowering others, and dedication to meaningful and transformative content have set new standards and inspired countless individuals. Oprah's legacy is one of empowerment, authenticity, and transformative influence, demonstrating the power of vision, resilience, and authenticity in achieving extraordinary success and making a significant impact.

Impact on Industry: Transforming Television and Media Landscapes

Oprah Winfrey's influence on the television industry, particularly daytime television, is unparalleled. When "The Oprah Winfrey Show" debuted nationally in 1986, it quickly became a cultural phenomenon, transforming the landscape of daytime TV. Oprah's approach to her show was revolutionary; she combined entertainment with profound, often life-changing content. Unlike other talk shows of the time, which primarily focused on sensationalism and conflict, Oprah introduced a format that emphasized personal growth, emotional healing, and meaningful conversations.

A New Kind of Talk Show

Oprah's empathetic and authentic interviewing style set her apart from other talk show hosts. She had an innate ability to connect with her guests and audience on a deep, personal level. Oprah's show covered a wide range of topics, from personal development and health to social issues and celebrity interviews. Her willingness to tackle difficult and often taboo subjects, such as sexual abuse, mental health, and racism, created a safe space for open dialogue and fostered greater understanding and empathy.

One of the most significant aspects of "The Oprah Winfrey Show" was its ability to influence public opinion and spark cultural conversations. For example, Oprah's public revelation of her own experiences with sexual abuse led to widespread discussions about the issue and encouraged many others to come forward with their stories. The show also brought attention to various social issues, such as the AIDS crisis, domestic violence, and child abuse, helping to raise awareness and inspire action.

Creating Cultural Moments

Oprah's show was known for its memorable and impactful moments, many of which have become ingrained in popular culture. From giving away cars to her audience with the iconic phrase "You get a car! You get a car!" to hosting powerful interviews with figures like Nelson Mandela and Michael Jackson, Oprah created television moments that resonated with millions of viewers.

One of the most notable episodes was Oprah's 1988 interview with author Toni Morrison, in which they discussed Morrison's novel "Beloved." The interview not only brought widespread attention to Morrison's work but also sparked a larger conversation about the representation of African American history and culture in literature. Oprah's ability to elevate important cultural conversations through her show demonstrated the power of television as a medium for social change.

Empowering Viewers

Oprah's emphasis on personal empowerment and self-improvement was a central theme of her show. She encouraged viewers to take control of their lives, pursue their dreams, and overcome personal challenges. Through segments like "Oprah's Book Club," "Oprah's Favorite Things," and "The Big Give,"

Oprah provided tools, resources, and inspiration for viewers to make positive changes in their lives.

"Oprah's Book Club," launched in 1996, had a profound impact on the publishing industry and reading habits. The club introduced millions of readers to a diverse range of authors and genres, promoting a love of reading and supporting the literary community. Many of the books selected for the club became bestsellers, and the club played a significant role in shaping literary trends and discussions.

Harpo Productions: A New Model for Media Ownership

Oprah's decision to form her own production company, Harpo Productions, in 1986 was a groundbreaking move that redefined media ownership and control. Harpo Productions gave Oprah full creative control over her content, allowing her to produce high-quality, impactful programming that reflected her values and vision. This level of autonomy was rare for women, particularly women of color, in the media industry at the time.

Harpo Productions quickly became a powerhouse in the entertainment industry, producing not only "The Oprah Winfrey Show" but also several successful spin-offs, including "Dr. Phil," "Rachael Ray," and "The Dr. Oz Show." These shows, which were produced by Harpo and hosted by personalities Oprah had mentored, further expanded her influence and solidified Harpo Productions' reputation as a leader in daytime television.

In addition to television, Harpo Productions ventured into film production, with notable projects such as "The Color Purple" (1985), in which Oprah made her acting debut, and "Beloved" (1998). These films, both of which received critical acclaim, demonstrated Harpo's ability to produce diverse and impactful content across multiple media platforms.

The Oprah Winfrey Network (OWN): Expanding the Vision

In January 2011, Oprah launched the Oprah Winfrey Network (OWN) in partnership with Discovery Communications. OWN was created to extend Oprah's mission of providing inspiring and empowering content beyond the format of a daily talk show. The network's programming includes a mix of talk shows, documentaries, reality TV, and original scripted series, all designed to uplift and enlighten viewers.

OWN's programming lineup reflects Oprah's commitment to meaningful and transformative content. Shows like "Super Soul Sunday," "Oprah's Master Class," and "Iyanla: Fix My Life" explore themes of spirituality, personal growth, and healing, resonating with viewers seeking inspiration and guidance. "Super Soul Sunday," in particular, features interviews with thought leaders, authors, and spiritual teachers, creating a platform for profound and insightful conversations.

OWN has also produced several successful original scripted series, including "Queen Sugar" and

"Greenleaf." These series, which focus on diverse and complex characters and stories, have received critical acclaim and a dedicated audience. "Queen Sugar," created by Ava DuVernay and executive produced by Oprah, explores themes of family, identity, and social justice, while "Greenleaf" delves into the secrets and scandals of a powerful African American church family.

Despite initial challenges and lower-than-expected ratings, Oprah's unwavering commitment to her vision and her ability to adapt and innovate have made OWN a respected and influential network. The network's focus on meaningful and transformative content has resonated with viewers, creating a loyal audience and a strong brand.

Lessons Learned: Authenticity and the Power of Personal Connection

Oprah Winfrey's success can be attributed to many factors, but two of the most important are her authenticity and her ability to connect personally with her audience. These qualities have not only defined her career but also provided valuable lessons for entrepreneurs, business leaders, and media professionals.

The Power of Authenticity

One of Oprah's most significant contributions to the media industry is her emphasis on authenticity. Throughout her career, Oprah has remained true to herself and her values, creating a brand that is synonymous with trust and integrity. Her authenticity has been a cornerstone of her success, resonating deeply with her audience and setting her apart from other media figures.

Oprah's authenticity is evident in her approach to storytelling and interviewing. She shares her own experiences and vulnerabilities, creating a space for others to do the same. By being open and honest about her own challenges and triumphs, Oprah has built a strong emotional connection with her audience, fostering trust and loyalty.

For example, Oprah's public revelation of her own experiences with sexual abuse on "The Oprah Winfrey Show" was a powerful and courageous act. By sharing her story, she not only helped to destigmatize the issue but also encouraged others to come forward with their experiences. Oprah's willingness to be vulnerable and authentic has created a safe space for important conversations and has had a profound impact on her audience.

Authenticity is not just about being open and honest; it is also about aligning actions with values. Oprah's commitment to meaningful and transformative content, her philanthropic efforts, and her dedication to empowering others all reflect her core values. This alignment has strengthened her brand and created a deep and lasting connection with her audience.

In today's business environment, authenticity is more important than ever. Consumers are increasingly looking for brands and leaders they can trust, and authenticity is a key factor in building that trust. Entrepreneurs and business leaders can learn from

Oprah's example by staying true to their values and being open and honest in their interactions. Authenticity not only builds trust and loyalty but also creates a strong and lasting connection with customers.

The Power of Personal Connection

Another fundamental lesson from Oprah Winfrey's journey is the importance of personal connection. Oprah's ability to connect with people on a deep and personal level has been a significant factor in her success. Her empathetic and compassionate approach to interviewing and storytelling has created a powerful bond with her audience.

Oprah's personal connection with her audience is evident in the way she engages with her guests and viewers. She listens actively, asks thoughtful questions, and responds with empathy and understanding. This approach not only creates a sense of intimacy and trust but also allows for deeper and more meaningful conversations.

For example, Oprah's interview with Michael Jackson in 1993 was one of the most-watched interviews in television history. Her ability to connect with Jackson and create a safe space for him to share his story resulted in an insightful and revealing conversation. Oprah's empathetic and compassionate approach allowed Jackson to open up in a way that he had not done before, creating a powerful and memorable television moment.

Oprah's ability to connect personally with her

audience extends beyond her interviews. Through initiatives like "Oprah's Book Club," "Oprah's Favorite Things," and the "Live Your Best Life" tour, Oprah has created opportunities for her audience to engage with her and each other in meaningful ways. These initiatives have fostered a sense of community and connection among her audience, reinforcing the bond they share with Oprah.

In today's business environment, personal connection is more important than ever. Consumers are increasingly looking for brands and leaders who understand and care about their needs and experiences. Entrepreneurs and business leaders can learn from Oprah's example by creating opportunities for personal connection with their customers and stakeholders. This connection not only builds trust and loyalty but also creates a positive and supportive community.

Empathy and Compassion

Empathy and compassion are central to Oprah's approach to media and storytelling. Her ability to understand and relate to the experiences of others has made her a powerful and influential figure. Oprah's empathetic approach to interviewing and storytelling has created a space for important conversations and promoted greater understanding and compassion.

Oprah's empathy is evident in her willingness to tackle difficult and often taboo subjects. From sexual abuse and mental health to race and gender, Oprah has used her platform to address important social issues and create a space for open and honest dialogue. Her empathetic approach has helped to destigmatize these issues and promote greater understanding and empathy.

For example, Oprah's series of shows on sexual abuse, including her own public revelation of her experiences, had a profound impact on the national conversation about the issue. Her empathetic and compassionate approach created a safe space for survivors to share their stories and encouraged others to come forward. Oprah's willingness to use her platform to address difficult issues has made a significant contribution to social change and awareness.

In today's business environment, empathy and compassion are more important than ever. Consumers are increasingly looking for brands and leaders who understand and care about their needs and experiences. Entrepreneurs and business leaders can learn from Oprah's example by creating a culture of empathy and compassion within their organizations. This approach not only builds trust and loyalty but also fosters a positive and supportive work environment.

Innovation and Adaptability

Oprah Winfrey's journey is also a testament to the power of innovation and adaptability. Throughout her career, Oprah has demonstrated an ability to anticipate and respond to changes in the media industry, positioning herself as a leader and innovator.

One of the key elements of Oprah's success is her willingness to take risks and explore new opportunities. From launching Harpo Productions to creating the Oprah Winfrey Network, Oprah has consistently pushed the boundaries of traditional media and created new and innovative platforms. Her ability to identify and capitalize on emerging trends has been a significant factor in her success.

Oprah's adaptability is also evident in her approach to content creation. She has consistently evolved her programming to reflect the changing needs and interests of her audience, from the talk show format of "The Oprah Winfrey Show" to the diverse and dynamic programming of the Oprah Winfrey Network. Oprah's ability to adapt and innovate has ensured her continued relevance and influence in the media industry.

In today's fast-paced business environment, innovation and adaptability are essential for success. Entrepreneurs and business leaders can learn from Oprah's example by staying attuned to market trends, being open to new ideas, and being willing to take calculated risks. Innovation is not just about creating new products or services; it is about finding new ways to meet the needs of customers and deliver value.

Leadership and Mentorship

Oprah Winfrey's leadership style is characterized by her focus on empowerment and mentorship. She believes in leading by example and providing guidance and support to those around her. Oprah's ability to inspire and empower others has been a significant factor in her success.

One of the key elements of Oprah's leadership strategy is her focus on positive reinforcement. She believes that recognizing and celebrating achievements is essential for motivating and retaining talent. The numerous recognition and incentive programs at Harpo Productions and the Oprah Winfrey Network reflect this philosophy.

Oprah's mentorship programs have also created opportunities for individuals to learn and grow under her guidance. Throughout her career, Oprah has mentored and supported numerous individuals, helping them to navigate the challenges of the media industry and achieve their goals. Her ability to provide guidance and support has created a positive and motivating environment for those around her.

In today's business environment, effective leadership and mentorship are more important than ever. Entrepreneurs and business leaders can learn from Oprah's example by creating a culture of empowerment and mentorship within their organizations. Empowering others and providing mentorship not only drives business success but also fosters a positive and supportive work environment.

Oprah Winfrey's remarkable journey and achievements have had a lasting impact on the television and media landscapes. Her innovative approach to storytelling, commitment to empowering others, and dedication to meaningful and transformative content have set new standards and inspired countless individuals. Oprah's legacy is one of empowerment, authenticity, and transformative influence, demonstrating the power of vision, resilience, and authenticity in achieving extraordinary success and making a significant impact.

Oprah's ability to connect personally with her audience, her emphasis on authenticity, and her commitment to empathy and compassion have created a powerful bond with her viewers and set her apart as a media powerhouse. Her innovative and adaptable approach to content creation and media ownership has ensured her continued relevance and influence in the industry.

As entrepreneurs and business leaders look to the future, there is much to learn from Oprah Winfrey's journey. By embracing authenticity, fostering personal connections, empowering others, and staying attuned to market trends, they can build strong, resilient brands that resonate with their audiences and make a meaningful impact. Oprah's story serves as an inspiration and a blueprint for those who aspire to make a lasting impact in their industries and the world.

Chapter 5: Martha Stewart - The Domestic Diva

Martha Stewart, born Martha Helen Kostyra on August 3, 1941, in Jersey City, New Jersey, grew up in Nutley, a working-class suburb. She was the second of six children in a family of Polish-American heritage. Her father, Edward Kostyra, was a pharmaceutical salesman, and her mother, Martha Ruszkowski Kostyra, was a schoolteacher and homemaker. It was in this home environment that Martha first developed her love for cooking, gardening, and homemaking—skills that would later become the foundation of her career.

Martha's parents played a crucial role in shaping her domestic skills. Her mother taught her how to cook and sew, while her father, an avid gardener, shared his knowledge of horticulture with her. These early lessons were not merely about household chores but were imparted with a sense of pride and perfectionism that Martha absorbed deeply. By the age of 10, Martha was already skilled in various domestic arts, and she often helped her family by organizing parties and creating elaborate meals.

During her teenage years, Martha began modeling to earn extra money, which helped her pay for her college education. She attended Barnard College in New York City, where she initially planned to major in chemistry but later switched to art, European history, and architectural history. While at Barnard, she continued modeling and appeared in several television commercials and print advertisements, which gave her early exposure to the world of media and entertainment.

In 1961, Martha married Andrew Stewart, a law student at Yale Law School. After graduating from Barnard in 1962, she worked as a stockbroker on Wall Street, a job that honed her business acumen and understanding of the financial markets. This experience was instrumental in developing the business skills she would later use to build her media empire. However, the domestic arts remained her true passion, and she continued to refine her skills in cooking, gardening, and home décor in her free time.

Martha and Andrew moved to Westport, Connecticut, in 1972, where they purchased and began renovating an old farmhouse. This project reignited Martha's passion for homemaking and entertaining. She started a catering business from her kitchen, which quickly became popular for its high-quality, beautifully presented dishes. Martha's catering business allowed her to combine her culinary skills with her flair for presentation and event planning, establishing her reputation as an expert in domestic arts.

Achievements: Building Martha Stewart Living Omnimedia into a Lifestyle Empire

Martha Stewart's journey from a successful caterer to a media mogul began in the late 1970s and early 1980s. Her attention to detail, commitment to quality, and ability to present ordinary tasks as extraordinary experiences set her apart from others in the industry. Martha's break came in 1982 when she published her first book, "Entertaining," which became a best-seller and solidified her reputation as an authority on domestic arts.

The Rise of Martha Stewart Living

"Entertaining" was more than just a cookbook; it was a comprehensive guide to hosting and entertaining, filled with beautiful photographs and detailed instructions. The book's success led to a series of additional publications, each focusing on different aspects of homemaking, including cooking, gardening, and decorating. Martha's ability to demystify complex tasks and present them in an accessible and appealing way resonated with readers, establishing her as a trusted source of domestic wisdom.

In 1990, Martha Stewart took her expertise to the next level by launching "Martha Stewart Living," a magazine dedicated to her vision of domestic perfection. The magazine featured a wide range of content, including recipes, gardening tips, home décor ideas, and holiday entertaining guides. It quickly became a must-read for homemakers and enthusiasts of the domestic arts, known for its high-quality photography and detailed, step-by-step instructions.

The success of "Martha Stewart Living" magazine laid the groundwork for Martha's media empire. Recognizing the potential to expand her brand across multiple platforms, Martha founded Martha Stewart Living Omnimedia (MSLO) in 1997. MSLO was designed to encompass all aspects of her brand, including publishing, broadcasting, merchandising, and digital media. This strategic move allowed Martha to maintain control over her brand and ensure consistency across all channels.

Television and Multimedia Expansion

Martha's foray into television began in the early 1990s with the launch of her first show, "Martha Stewart Living," which aired weekly on CBS. The show brought her magazine's content to life, with Martha demonstrating recipes, craft projects, gardening tips, and home décor ideas. Her calm, methodical teaching style and attention to detail made the show a hit, further solidifying her reputation as the ultimate domestic guru.

The success of "Martha Stewart Living" on television opened the door for additional programming, including holiday specials and themed series. Martha's ability to seamlessly transition between different media formats showcased her versatility and broadened her audience. She also made frequent guest appearances on popular talk shows and news programs, further increasing her visibility and influence.

In addition to television, MSLO expanded into radio and digital media. Martha Stewart Living Radio launched on SiriusXM in 2005, offering a platform for Martha and her team to share tips and advice on various topics related to home and lifestyle. The company's digital presence grew with the launch of MarthaStewart.com, a comprehensive website featuring articles, videos, and interactive content.

Publishing and Product Lines

Publishing remained a core component of Martha Stewart's business strategy. In addition to "Martha Stewart Living" magazine, MSLO published several other successful titles, including "Martha Stewart Weddings" and "Everyday Food." Each publication catered to a specific audience and reinforced Martha's brand as the go-to source for all things related to homemaking and entertaining.

Martha's influence extended into the retail sector with the launch of various product lines bearing her name. In partnership with Kmart, she introduced a line of home goods, including cookware, bedding, and décor items. The products were designed to reflect Martha's aesthetic and quality standards, making her signature style accessible to a broader audience. The partnership was a significant success, generating substantial revenue and expanding Martha's brand into the mainstream retail market.

Subsequent partnerships with other major retailers, such as Macy's, Home Depot, and Michaels, further expanded Martha's product offerings. These collaborations included lines of furniture, craft supplies, garden tools, and pet products, all designed with Martha's meticulous attention to detail. Each product line was accompanied by extensive marketing campaigns and in-store displays, reinforcing the connection between the products and Martha's brand.

Overcoming Challenges and Legal Battles

Martha Stewart's career has not been without its

challenges. In 2001, she became embroiled in a legal battle related to insider trading allegations involving her sale of ImClone Systems stock. In 2004, she was convicted of conspiracy, obstruction of justice, and making false statements to federal investigators. Martha served a five-month prison sentence, followed by five months of home confinement.

Despite the setback, Martha's resilience and determination allowed her to stage a remarkable comeback. During her time in prison, she maintained her focus on her business and began planning her return. Upon her release in 2005, Martha resumed her role at MSLO and launched a new television show, "The Martha Stewart Show," which aired on the Hallmark Channel.

Martha's ability to navigate the legal challenges and rebuild her brand demonstrated her unwavering commitment to her vision. She continued to expand her media empire, leveraging her expertise and reputation to regain the trust and admiration of her audience. The experience also highlighted her strength and resilience, qualities that have been integral to her success.

Legacy and Influence

Martha Stewart's impact on the domestic arts and lifestyle industry is profound and far-reaching. She has transformed the way people approach cooking, gardening, entertaining, and home décor, elevating these activities to an art form. Her emphasis on quality, attention to detail, and commitment to excellence have set new standards in the industry.

Martha's influence extends beyond her media and product offerings. She has inspired countless individuals to take pride in their homes and embrace the joy of creating beautiful and functional spaces. Her ability to demystify complex tasks and present them in an accessible and appealing way has empowered people to explore their creativity and develop new skills.

In addition to her contributions to the domestic arts, Martha Stewart has been a trailblazer for women in business. She has demonstrated that it is possible to build a successful, multifaceted career while maintaining a commitment to quality and integrity. Her journey from a caterer to a media mogul serves as an inspiration to aspiring entrepreneurs and business leaders.

Philanthropy and Community Involvement

Martha Stewart has also been actively involved in philanthropy and community service. She has supported various charitable organizations and initiatives, particularly those related to education, healthcare, and the arts. Martha's commitment to giving back reflects her belief in the importance of using her platform and resources to make a positive impact on society.

One notable example of her philanthropic efforts is the Martha Stewart Center for Living at Mount Sinai Hospital in New York City. The center, established in 2007, focuses on geriatric care and aims to improve the quality of life for older adults through comprehensive medical services, research, and education. Martha's support for the center underscores her dedication to enhancing the well-being of individuals and communities.

Martha Stewart's remarkable journey from a modest upbringing in New Jersey to building a lifestyle empire is a testament to her vision, resilience, and dedication. Her ability to transform ordinary domestic tasks into extraordinary experiences has made her a beloved and influential figure in the domestic arts and lifestyle industry. Through her media ventures, product lines, and philanthropic efforts, Martha has left an indelible mark on the world, inspiring countless individuals to embrace the art of homemaking and pursue their passions with confidence and creativity.

Martha Stewart's legacy is one of excellence, innovation, and empowerment. Her unwavering commitment to quality and her ability to adapt and evolve in the face of challenges have set new standards in the industry. As a pioneer in media and business, Martha has paved the way for future generations of entrepreneurs and business leaders, demonstrating that with vision, hard work, and resilience, it is possible to achieve extraordinary success and make a lasting impact.

Impact on Industry: Shaping the Modern Lifestyle and Home Improvement Sectors

Martha Stewart's influence on the modern lifestyle and home improvement sectors cannot be overstated. From her early days as a caterer to becoming a global brand, Martha has transformed how people think about cooking, gardening, decorating, and entertaining. Her approach to domestic arts has elevated these activities to a level of sophistication and accessibility, making them both desirable and achievable for a broad audience.

Martha's vision was to make everyday life more beautiful, functional, and enjoyable. She believed that everyone could create a home environment that was both practical and aesthetically pleasing. Through her books, magazines, television shows, and product lines, Martha provided the knowledge, inspiration, and tools needed to achieve this vision.

Publishing and Media: Building an Empire of Inspiration

One of Martha Stewart's most significant contributions to the lifestyle and home improvement sectors is her extensive body of published work. Her first book, "Entertaining," published in 1982, set the tone for what would become a prolific career in publishing. The book was a comprehensive guide to hosting and entertaining, filled with beautiful photographs and detailed instructions that made even the most complex tasks seem manageable.

"Entertaining" was followed by a series of best-selling books covering various aspects of homemaking, including "Martha Stewart's Quick Cook," "Martha Stewart's Hors d'Oeuvres," and "Martha Stewart's Christmas." Each book was meticulously crafted, reflecting Martha's commitment to quality and attention to detail. Her ability to present sophisticated concepts in an accessible way resonated with readers, establishing her as a trusted authority in domestic arts.

In 1990, Martha launched "Martha Stewart Living" magazine, which became a cornerstone of her media empire. The magazine featured a wide range of content, including recipes, gardening tips, home décor ideas, and holiday entertaining guides. It quickly became a must-read for homemakers and enthusiasts of the domestic arts, known for its high-quality photography and detailed, step-by-step instructions.

The success of "Martha Stewart Living" magazine led to the launch of additional publications, including "Martha Stewart Weddings" and "Everyday Food." Each publication catered to a specific audience and reinforced Martha's brand as the go-to source for all things related to homemaking and entertaining. Martha's influence extended beyond print media, as she became a regular guest on popular talk shows and news programs, further increasing her visibility and impact.

Television: Bringing Domestic Arts to Life

Martha Stewart's foray into television began in the early 1990s with the launch of her first show, "Martha Stewart Living," which aired weekly on CBS. The show brought her magazine's content to life, with Martha demonstrating recipes, craft projects, gardening tips, and home décor ideas. Her calm, methodical teaching style and attention to detail made the show a hit, further solidifying her reputation as the ultimate domestic guru.

The success of "Martha Stewart Living" on television opened the door for additional programming, including holiday specials and themed series. Martha's ability to seamlessly transition between different media formats showcased her versatility and broadened her audience. She also made frequent guest appearances on popular talk shows and news programs, further increasing her visibility and influence.

Martha's television presence expanded with the launch of "The Martha Stewart Show" in 2005. The daily show aired on the Hallmark Channel and featured a mix of cooking, crafting, gardening, and home improvement segments. The show provided a platform for Martha to share her expertise with a broader audience and introduced new generations to the joys of homemaking and entertaining.

Product Lines: Bringing Martha's Vision to Life

Martha Stewart's influence extended into the retail sector with the launch of various product lines bearing her name. In partnership with Kmart, she introduced a line of home goods, including cookware, bedding, and décor items. The products were designed to reflect Martha's aesthetic and quality standards, making her signature style accessible to a broader audience. The partnership was a significant success, generating substantial revenue and expanding Martha's brand into the mainstream retail market.

Subsequent partnerships with other major retailers,

such as Macy's, Home Depot, and Michaels, further expanded Martha's product offerings. These collaborations included lines of furniture, craft supplies, garden tools, and pet products, all designed with Martha's meticulous attention to detail. Each product line was accompanied by extensive marketing campaigns and in-store displays, reinforcing the connection between the products and Martha's brand.

Martha's product lines have had a profound impact on the home improvement and lifestyle sectors. By making high-quality, beautifully designed products accessible to a wide audience, she has empowered people to create functional and aesthetically pleasing homes. Her emphasis on quality and design has set new standards for the industry, influencing other brands to elevate their offerings and meet the expectations of discerning consumers.

Digital Media: Embracing New Technologies

As digital media began to rise, Martha Stewart Living Omnimedia (MSLO) embraced new technologies to reach a broader audience. The launch of MarthaStewart.com provided a comprehensive online resource for homemaking and entertaining, featuring articles, videos, and interactive content. The website became a valuable extension of Martha's brand, offering users access to her expertise and inspiration at their fingertips.

Martha's digital presence expanded with the launch of apps, social media channels, and online tutorials. These platforms allowed her to connect with a younger, tech-savvy audience and adapt to the changing media landscape. By embracing digital media, Martha ensured that her brand remained relevant and accessible in an increasingly digital world.

Shaping Trends and Influencing Consumers

Martha Stewart's influence on lifestyle and home improvement extends beyond her media and product offerings. She has played a pivotal role in shaping trends and influencing consumer behavior. Her emphasis on quality, attention to detail, and commitment to excellence have set new standards in the industry.

Martha's ability to anticipate and shape trends has been a key factor in her success. Whether it's the resurgence of DIY crafts, the popularity of farm-to-table cooking, or the emphasis on sustainable living, Martha has been at the forefront of these movements. Her ability to identify emerging trends and present them in an accessible and appealing way has made her a trendsetter in the lifestyle and home improvement sectors.

Martha's influence is also evident in the growing popularity of homemaking and domestic arts as hobbies and passions. By presenting these activities as enjoyable and fulfilling, she has inspired countless individuals to explore their creativity and develop new skills. Martha's impact on the industry is not just about the products she sells or the content she creates; it's about the inspiration and empowerment she provides to her audience.

Lessons Learned: Diversification and Brand Consistency

One of the fundamental lessons from Martha Stewart's career is the importance of diversification. Martha's ability to expand her brand across multiple platforms and product categories has been a key factor in her success. By diversifying her offerings, she has been able to reach a broader audience, mitigate risks, and create new revenue streams.

Expanding Across Media Platforms

Martha's media empire began with her first book, "Entertaining," and quickly expanded to include magazines, television shows, and digital content. Each platform allowed her to reach different segments of her audience and provide them with valuable content in various formats. The success of "Martha Stewart Living" magazine led to the launch of additional publications, such as "Martha Stewart Weddings" and "Everyday Food," each catering to a specific audience.

Television became a significant part of Martha's brand, with shows like "Martha Stewart Living" and "The Martha Stewart Show" bringing her expertise to life. These shows provided a visual and interactive way for audiences to engage with Martha's content, further solidifying her reputation as an authority in domestic arts.

The launch of MarthaStewart.com and the embrace of digital media allowed Martha to connect with a younger, tech-savvy audience. By expanding her brand across multiple media platforms, Martha was able to reach a broader audience and provide them with valuable content in the format that suited them best.

Entering the Retail Market

Martha's foray into the retail market with product lines bearing her name was another successful example of diversification. Her partnerships with major retailers like Kmart, Macy's, Home Depot, and Michaels allowed her to bring her vision to life through high-quality, beautifully designed products. These collaborations not only generated substantial revenue but also expanded her brand into new markets.

The success of Martha's product lines demonstrated the power of brand extension and diversification. By offering a wide range of products, from cookware and bedding to furniture and craft supplies, Martha was able to meet the diverse needs of her audience and create new opportunities for growth.

Venturing into New Categories

Martha's ability to diversify extended beyond traditional media and retail. She ventured into new categories, such as food and beverage, with the launch of Martha Stewart-branded wines, meal kits, and pet products. Each new category was carefully selected to align with her brand and provide value to her audience.

Martha's diversification strategy has been successful because it is rooted in a deep understanding of her audience and their needs. By expanding her brand into new categories, she has been able to stay relevant and continue to grow her business in an ever-changing market.

The Importance of Brand Consistency

While diversification has been a key factor in Martha Stewart's success, it has been equally important to maintain brand consistency. Martha's brand is built on a foundation of quality, attention to detail, and a commitment to excellence. Ensuring that these values are reflected in every aspect of her brand has been essential for building trust and loyalty among her audience.

Maintaining Quality Across All Offerings

One of the hallmarks of Martha Stewart's brand is her unwavering commitment to quality. Whether it's a recipe, a magazine article, a television segment, or a product, Martha ensures that everything bearing her name meets the highest standards. This commitment to quality has been a key factor in building trust and credibility with her audience.

Martha's attention to detail is evident in every aspect of her brand. From the design of her products to the presentation of her content, she ensures that everything is meticulously crafted and presented. This level of detail not only enhances the user experience but also reinforces the perception of quality and excellence.

Consistent Brand Messaging

Maintaining consistent brand messaging has also been crucial for Martha Stewart's success. Her brand is synonymous with domestic arts, homemaking, and entertaining, and this message is consistently communicated across all platforms and product categories. Whether it's a magazine article, a television segment, or a product advertisement, the messaging reinforces the core values of Martha's brand.

Martha's ability to maintain consistent brand messaging has been essential for building a strong and recognizable brand. Consistency in messaging creates a cohesive brand identity, which helps to build trust and loyalty among consumers.

Aligning Brand Values with Consumer Expectations

Martha Stewart's brand is built on a foundation of values, including quality, authenticity, and a commitment to excellence. Ensuring that these values are consistently reflected in her offerings has been essential for meeting consumer expectations and building a loyal audience.

Martha's brand values are evident in her emphasis on quality and attention to detail. Her ability to present complex tasks in an accessible and appealing way reflects her commitment to making domestic arts enjoyable and fulfilling. By aligning her brand values with consumer expectations, Martha has been able to create a strong and loyal audience.

Adapting to Changing Market Trends

While maintaining brand consistency is important, it is also essential to adapt to changing market trends. Martha Stewart's ability to anticipate and respond to trends has been a key factor in her success. Whether it's the rise of digital media, the growing popularity of DIY crafts, or the emphasis on sustainable living, Martha has been able to stay ahead of the curve and ensure that her brand remains relevant.

Martha's ability to adapt to changing market trends while maintaining brand consistency is a testament to her vision and leadership. By staying attuned to market trends and consumer needs, she has been able to continue to grow her brand and create new opportunities for success.

Martha Stewart's impact on the modern lifestyle and home improvement sectors is profound and far-reaching. Her ability to elevate domestic arts to a level of sophistication and accessibility has transformed how people approach cooking, gardening, decorating, and entertaining. Through her books, magazines, television shows, product lines, and digital content, Martha has provided the knowledge, inspiration, and tools needed to create beautiful and functional homes.

The lessons learned from Martha Stewart's career are invaluable for entrepreneurs and business leaders. Her emphasis on diversification and brand consistency has been a key factor in her success. By expanding her brand across multiple platforms and product categories, Martha has been able to reach a broader audience, mitigate risks, and create new revenue streams. At the same time, her unwavering commitment to quality and attention to detail has ensured that her brand remains strong and trusted.

Martha Stewart's legacy is one of excellence, innovation, and empowerment. Her ability to adapt to changing market trends while maintaining brand consistency is a testament to her vision and leadership. As a pioneer in media and business, Martha has paved the way for future generations of entrepreneurs and business leaders, demonstrating that with vision, hard work, and resilience, it is possible to achieve extraordinary success and make a lasting impact.

Chapter 6: Meg Whitman - The E-Commerce Innovator

Margaret Cushing Whitman, better known as Meg Whitman, was born on August 4, 1956, in Cold Spring Harbor, New York. Raised in an affluent family, Whitman was encouraged to pursue education and excellence from a young age. Her father, Hendricks Whitman, was a successful businessman, and her mother, Margaret Whitman, was a stay-at-home mom who instilled strong values of hard work and determination in her children.

Meg Whitman excelled academically and attended the prestigious Princeton University, where she graduated with a degree in economics in 1977. Her interest in business and economics led her to Harvard Business School, where she earned her MBA in 1979. These formative years at two of the nation's most elite educational institutions set the stage for her future career in the business world.

Whitman began her professional career at Procter & Gamble as a brand manager, where she gained valuable experience in marketing and consumer goods. Her time at Procter & Gamble taught her the importance of brand management, strategic planning, and consumer engagement, skills that would prove invaluable in her later roles. After Procter & Gamble, she worked at Bain & Company, a global management consulting firm, where she further honed her skills in business strategy and operations.

In the late 1980s, Whitman transitioned into the technology sector, taking on senior roles at several prominent companies. She served as vice president of strategic planning at The Walt Disney Company, where she was involved in the development of new business opportunities and strategic initiatives. Her success at Disney led to her appointment as president of the children's entertainment division at Stride Rite Corporation, where she oversaw the development and marketing of the company's product lines.

Whitman's career in technology took a significant leap forward when she joined the fledgling internet company eBay in 1998. At the time, eBay was a relatively unknown start-up with just 30 employees and a fledgling user base. Whitman's appointment as CEO marked the beginning of a transformative period for the company and the e-commerce industry as a whole.

Achievements: Transforming eBay into a Global E-Commerce Giant

When Meg Whitman took the helm of eBay in March 1998, the company was generating around $4 million in annual revenue. Founded in 1995 by Pierre Omidyar, eBay was a novel online auction site where individuals could buy and sell a variety of goods. Although the platform had shown potential, it lacked the infrastructure, strategy, and leadership needed to scale into a major business.

Whitman's arrival at eBay marked the beginning of a remarkable transformation. She brought a disciplined, strategic approach to the company, focusing on scaling operations, enhancing the user experience, and expanding the platform's reach. Under her leadership, eBay grew exponentially, becoming one of the most successful e-commerce companies in the world.

Strategic Vision and Leadership

One of Whitman's first actions as CEO was to create a clear strategic vision for eBay. She recognized that the company's success depended on its ability to create a safe, reliable, and user-friendly platform for buyers and sellers. To achieve this, she focused on several key areas:

- Scalability and Infrastructure: Whitman invested heavily in eBay's technological infrastructure to ensure that the platform could handle rapid growth. This included upgrading servers, improving the website's performance, and enhancing security measures. By building a robust infrastructure, Whitman ensured that eBay could support a growing user base and increased transaction volume.

- User Experience: Whitman placed a strong emphasis on improving the user experience for both buyers and sellers. She introduced features such as user feedback systems, which allowed buyers and sellers to rate each other, thereby building trust within the eBay community. This focus on trust and transparency was crucial in establishing eBay as a reliable and reputable platform.

- Global Expansion: Recognizing the potential for international growth, Whitman spearheaded eBay's expansion into new markets. She established operations in key international markets, including Europe, Asia, and Latin America, making eBay a truly global platform. This expansion not only increased eBay's user base but also diversified its revenue streams.

- Acquisitions and Partnerships: Whitman pursued strategic acquisitions and partnerships to enhance eBay's capabilities and expand its offerings. Notable acquisitions included PayPal, the online payment platform, which provided a seamless and secure payment solution for eBay users. This acquisition was instrumental in driving eBay's growth and enhancing the overall user experience.

Building a Community and Brand

One of Whitman's most significant achievements at eBay was her ability to build a strong sense of community among users. She understood that eBay's success depended on the trust and engagement of its user base. To foster this sense of community, Whitman implemented several key initiatives:

- User Engagement: Whitman prioritized user engagement and feedback, actively seeking input from buyers and sellers to improve the platform. She held regular town hall meetings, attended user conferences, and encouraged open communication between eBay's leadership and its users. This approach helped build a loyal and engaged community.

- Brand Development: Whitman invested in building eBay's brand as a trusted and reliable marketplace. Through strategic marketing campaigns and partnerships, she positioned eBay as the go-to platform for buying and selling a wide range of goods. The company's tagline, "Whatever it is, you can get it on eBay," became synonymous with the platform's vast and diverse offerings.

- Corporate Culture: Whitman fostered a positive corporate culture at eBay, emphasizing values such as trust, integrity, and customer focus. She believed that a strong corporate culture was essential for attracting and retaining top talent and for maintaining the company's reputation. Under her leadership, eBay became known for its innovative and collaborative work environment.

Financial Performance and Market Growth

Under Meg Whitman's leadership, eBay experienced extraordinary financial growth. The company's revenue grew from $4 million in 1998 to over $8 billion by the time she stepped down as CEO in 2008. This remarkable growth was driven by several factors:

- Increasing User Base: eBay's user base grew from around half a million users in 1998 to over 84 million active users by 2008. This rapid expansion was fueled by the platform's user-friendly interface, enhanced security measures, and global reach.

- Transaction Volume: The volume of transactions on eBay increased exponentially during Whitman's tenure. The platform facilitated millions of transactions daily, generating substantial revenue through listing fees, final value fees, and other service charges.

- Diversification of Revenue Streams: Whitman successfully diversified eBay's revenue streams through strategic acquisitions and partnerships. The acquisition of PayPal, in particular, was a game-changer, providing eBay with a reliable and scalable payment solution that became a significant revenue driver.

- Stock Performance: eBay's stock price reflected the company's impressive growth and market performance. Under Whitman's leadership, eBay's market capitalization grew from $600 million to over $40 billion, making it one of the most valuable technology companies in the world.

Challenges and Resilience

Whitman's tenure at eBay was not without challenges. The rapid growth of the company brought operational complexities, and the evolving competitive landscape required constant innovation and adaptation. Whitman's ability to navigate these challenges and maintain eBay's growth trajectory was a testament to her resilience and leadership.

- Operational Challenges: Scaling eBay's operations to accommodate rapid growth presented significant challenges. Whitman addressed these challenges by investing in technology and infrastructure, streamlining processes, and enhancing customer support. Her focus on operational excellence ensured that eBay could handle increased transaction volume and user activity.

- Competitive Pressure: As the e-commerce landscape evolved, eBay faced increasing competition from other online marketplaces and retail giants like Amazon. Whitman's strategic acquisitions, such as PayPal, and her emphasis on user experience helped eBay maintain its competitive edge. She also explored new business models and revenue streams to stay ahead of the competition.

- Regulatory and Legal Issues: eBay's global expansion brought regulatory and legal challenges, including issues related to cross-border trade, taxation, and consumer protection. Whitman worked closely with regulatory authorities and industry stakeholders to address these challenges and ensure compliance with local laws and regulations.

Legacy and Impact

Meg Whitman's legacy at eBay is one of transformation and innovation. Her strategic vision, leadership, and ability to execute complex initiatives turned eBay from a fledgling start-up into a global e-commerce giant. Whitman's impact on the industry extends beyond eBay, as her leadership principles and business strategies have influenced countless other technology companies and entrepreneurs.

- E-Commerce Innovation: Whitman's tenure at eBay demonstrated the potential of e-commerce to revolutionize the retail industry. Her emphasis on user experience, trust, and community-building set new standards for online marketplaces. eBay's success under her leadership paved the way for other e-commerce platforms to emerge and thrive.

- Women in Leadership: As one of the few female CEOs in the technology sector, Whitman broke barriers and served as a role model for women in business. Her success at eBay challenged traditional gender norms and demonstrated that women could lead and excel in male-dominated industries. Whitman's advocacy for diversity and inclusion continues to inspire future generations of women leaders.

- Strategic Acquisitions: Whitman's strategic acquisitions, particularly the purchase of PayPal, have had a lasting impact on the e-commerce industry. PayPal's integration with eBay provided a seamless and secure payment solution that has become a standard in online transactions. The success of this acquisition highlighted the importance of strategic partnerships and innovation in driving business growth.

- Leadership Principles: Whitman's leadership principles, including her focus on strategic vision, user experience, and operational excellence, have influenced countless business leaders and entrepreneurs. Her approach to building a strong corporate culture, fostering innovation, and prioritizing customer needs continues to be a model for successful leadership in the technology sector.

Lessons Learned: Diversification and Brand Consistency

Meg Whitman's success at eBay can be attributed in part to her strategic approach to diversification. By expanding eBay's offerings and entering new markets, Whitman ensured that the company could sustain its growth and remain competitive in a rapidly evolving industry.

Expanding Product Categories

One of Whitman's key strategies was to diversify eBay's product categories. Initially, eBay was primarily known as an online auction site for collectibles and used items. Whitman recognized the potential to expand the platform's offerings to include a broader range of products, from electronics and fashion to home goods and vehicles.

This diversification strategy not only attracted a wider audience but also increased the volume and value of transactions on the platform. By offering a diverse range of products, eBay became a one-stop-shop for consumers, enhancing its appeal and competitiveness.

Global Expansion

Whitman spearheaded eBay's global expansion, establishing operations in key international markets. This expansion strategy involved entering new countries, adapting the platform to local markets, and navigating regulatory and cultural differences. By diversifying geographically, eBay was able to tap into new user bases and revenue streams, mitigating the risks associated with reliance on a single market.

Global expansion also provided opportunities for cross-border trade, allowing users to buy and sell items internationally. This increased the platform's transaction volume and enhanced its value proposition for users.

Strategic Acquisitions

Under Whitman's leadership, eBay pursued strategic acquisitions to diversify its offerings and enhance its capabilities. The acquisition of PayPal in 2002 was a landmark deal that transformed eBay's payment processing capabilities. PayPal provided a secure and convenient payment solution for eBay users, addressing one of the platform's key pain points.

Other notable acquisitions included Half.com, an online marketplace for books, music, and movies, and StubHub, a ticket resale platform. These acquisitions allowed eBay to enter new markets and offer additional services, further diversifying its revenue streams.

New Business Models

Whitman explored new business models to diversify eBay's revenue streams and enhance its value proposition. One such model was the introduction of fixed-price listings alongside traditional auctions. This change allowed sellers to list items at a set price, appealing to buyers who preferred the certainty of a fixed price over the uncertainty of an auction.

The fixed-price model complemented eBay's auction format, attracting a broader range of sellers and buyers. This diversification of business models increased transaction volume and provided users with more options, enhancing the overall user experience.

The Importance of Brand Consistency

While diversification was crucial for eBay's growth, Whitman also understood the importance of maintaining brand consistency. Ensuring that eBay's core values and brand identity were reflected across all offerings and markets was essential for building trust and loyalty among users.

Building a Trusted Brand

Whitman recognized that trust was a cornerstone of eBay's success. She implemented measures to enhance security, protect users, and ensure a safe and reliable marketplace. The introduction of user feedback systems, buyer and seller protection programs, and secure payment options like PayPal all contributed to building a trusted brand.

Maintaining brand consistency required a commitment to upholding these values across all markets and product categories. Whitman ensured that eBay's core principles of trust, transparency, and customer focus were integrated into every aspect of the business, from product development to customer support.

Consistent User Experience

Delivering a consistent user experience was another key aspect of brand consistency. Whitman prioritized user experience enhancements, ensuring that the platform was user-friendly, intuitive, and reliable. This included investing in technology and infrastructure to support seamless transactions, improve website performance, and enhance security measures.

Consistency in user experience also involved adapting the platform to meet the needs of different markets while maintaining a cohesive brand identity. This balance of localization and consistency was crucial for building a global brand that resonated with users worldwide.

Unified Brand Messaging

Unified brand messaging was essential for reinforcing eBay's brand identity and values. Whitman ensured that eBay's marketing campaigns, communications, and user interactions consistently conveyed the company's commitment to trust, transparency, and customer focus.

Whether through advertising, public relations, or user engagement, eBay's messaging consistently emphasized the platform's value proposition and core principles. This unified approach to brand messaging helped build a strong and recognizable brand that resonated with users and stakeholders.

Cultural Alignment

Whitman fostered a positive corporate culture at eBay, emphasizing values such as trust, integrity, and customer focus. She believed that a strong corporate culture was essential for attracting and retaining top talent and for maintaining the company's reputation.

By aligning eBay's corporate culture with its brand values, Whitman ensured that employees were committed to upholding the company's principles and delivering on its promises. This cultural alignment was crucial for maintaining brand consistency and building a strong, cohesive organization.
Conclusion

Meg Whitman's remarkable journey from a brand manager at Procter & Gamble to the CEO of eBay is a testament to her strategic vision, leadership, and ability to execute complex initiatives. Her tenure at eBay transformed the company from a fledgling start-up into a global e-commerce giant, setting new standards for the industry and influencing countless other technology companies and entrepreneurs.

Whitman's strategic approach to diversification and

brand consistency was instrumental in eBay's success. By expanding the company's offerings, entering new markets, and pursuing strategic acquisitions, she ensured that eBay could sustain its growth and remain competitive in a rapidly evolving industry. At the same time, her commitment to maintaining brand consistency built trust and loyalty among users, reinforcing eBay's reputation as a trusted and reliable marketplace.

Meg Whitman's legacy at eBay is one of innovation, resilience, and transformative leadership. Her impact on the e-commerce industry extends beyond eBay, as her leadership principles and business strategies continue to inspire future generations of business leaders and entrepreneurs. Whitman's journey demonstrates that with vision, determination, and a focus on core values, it is possible to achieve extraordinary success and make a lasting impact on the world.

Impact on Industry: Setting Standards for Online Marketplaces

Meg Whitman's leadership at eBay not only transformed the company but also set new standards for the entire e-commerce industry. Under her guidance, eBay became a model for online marketplaces, pioneering practices and technologies that are now industry standards. Whitman's vision and strategic initiatives played a crucial role in shaping how online marketplaces operate today, influencing everything from user experience and security to global expansion and community building.

Creating a User-Centric Marketplace

When Meg Whitman joined eBay as CEO in 1998, she recognized that the key to success lay in creating a user-centric marketplace that prioritized the needs and experiences of its buyers and sellers. This focus on user experience became a cornerstone of eBay's strategy and set a precedent for other online marketplaces.

- User Feedback System: One of Whitman's first major initiatives was the implementation of a robust user feedback system. This system allowed buyers and sellers to rate each other and leave feedback on transactions. The feedback system introduced a level of transparency and trust that was crucial for the platform's success. It empowered users to make informed decisions and built a sense of accountability within the eBay community.

- Buyer and Seller Protections: To further enhance trust and security, Whitman introduced buyer and seller protection programs. These programs offered guarantees and dispute resolution mechanisms, ensuring that users could transact with confidence. By providing these protections, eBay established itself as a safe and reliable platform, encouraging more users to participate in online commerce.

- User-Friendly Interface: Whitman invested in improving eBay's user interface, making it more intuitive and accessible. Enhancements to the website's design and navigation helped users easily find products, list items for sale, and complete transactions. This focus on user-friendliness set a standard for online marketplaces, emphasizing the importance of seamless and enjoyable user experiences.

Innovations in Payment Solutions

One of the significant challenges for online marketplaces in the early days of e-commerce was ensuring secure and efficient payment processing. Under Whitman's leadership, eBay addressed this challenge through the strategic acquisition of PayPal in 2002. The integration of PayPal into eBay's platform was a game-changer, providing a reliable and convenient payment solution for users.

- Secure Transactions: PayPal offered a secure way for buyers and sellers to transact without sharing sensitive financial information. This security was crucial for building trust in the online marketplace and protecting users from fraud and theft. The integration of PayPal set a new standard for payment security in e-commerce.

- Seamless Integration: The seamless integration of PayPal with eBay's platform made the payment process quick and easy for users. This convenience encouraged more transactions and reduced barriers to buying and selling online. PayPal's user-friendly interface and robust security features became benchmarks for other payment solutions in the industry.

- Global Reach: PayPal's global presence and ability to handle multiple currencies facilitated eBay's international expansion. Users from different countries could easily transact on the platform, broadening eBay's reach and increasing its user base. This global payment solution set a precedent for other online marketplaces looking to expand internationally.

Building a Global Community

Whitman's vision for eBay extended beyond the United States. She saw the potential for eBay to become a global marketplace, connecting buyers and sellers from around the world. Under her leadership, eBay embarked on an ambitious international expansion strategy, establishing operations in key markets across Europe, Asia, and Latin America.

- Localized Marketplaces: To cater to the unique needs of different regions, eBay established localized marketplaces with country-specific websites and support. This localization strategy allowed eBay to tailor its offerings to local preferences and cultural nuances, making the platform more appealing to international users.

- Cross-Border Trade: Whitman championed cross-border trade, enabling users to buy and sell items internationally. This expanded the range of products available on the platform and opened up new opportunities for sellers to reach global audiences. eBay's cross-border trade initiatives set a standard for other marketplaces, demonstrating the benefits of facilitating international commerce.

- Community Building: Whitman emphasized the importance of building a strong sense of community among eBay users. She fostered user engagement through forums, events, and feedback mechanisms, creating a loyal and active user base. This focus on community building became a hallmark of successful online marketplaces, highlighting the importance of fostering connections and trust among users.

Innovative Business Models

Under Whitman's leadership, eBay pioneered several innovative business models that have since become industry standards. These models enhanced the platform's appeal and diversified its revenue streams, ensuring sustained growth and competitiveness.

- Fixed-Price Listings: While eBay was initially known for its auction format, Whitman introduced fixed-price listings to attract a broader range of buyers and sellers. This hybrid model allowed users to choose between auctions and fixed prices, catering to different preferences and increasing transaction volume. The introduction of fixed-price listings set a precedent for other marketplaces, highlighting the importance of offering diverse selling options.

- Vertical Marketplaces: Whitman recognized the potential for eBay to cater to specific niches and vertical markets. The company launched specialized marketplaces for categories like motors, real estate, and collectibles, providing tailored experiences for users interested in these areas. This focus on vertical marketplaces demonstrated the value of catering to niche markets and creating specialized platforms within a broader marketplace.

- Advertising and Promotions: To diversify revenue streams, Whitman introduced advertising and promotional opportunities on eBay. Sellers could pay for enhanced visibility through sponsored listings and banner ads, while eBay generated additional revenue from advertising fees. This monetization strategy became a standard for online marketplaces, highlighting the potential for advertising revenue in e-commerce.

Lessons Learned: Strategic Growth and Adaptability

Meg Whitman's success at eBay was rooted in her ability to balance strategic growth with the company's core values. Her approach to scaling the business was methodical and focused, ensuring that eBay could sustain its rapid expansion without compromising on user experience or trust.

Prioritizing User Experience

One of Whitman's key principles was prioritizing user

experience as the foundation for growth. She believed that a positive and seamless user experience was essential for attracting and retaining customers, driving transactions, and building a loyal community.

- Continuous Improvement: Whitman implemented a culture of continuous improvement at eBay, encouraging teams to constantly seek ways to enhance the platform and address user feedback. This iterative approach ensured that eBay could adapt to changing user needs and preferences, maintaining a high level of user satisfaction.

- Data-Driven Decisions: Under Whitman's leadership, eBay leveraged data and analytics to inform strategic decisions. By analyzing user behavior, transaction patterns, and feedback, the company could identify areas for improvement and make informed choices about product development, marketing, and expansion.

- Customer Support: Whitman recognized the importance of providing excellent customer support to build trust and loyalty. eBay invested in robust customer support infrastructure, including help centers, forums, and dedicated support teams. This commitment to customer service set a standard for other online marketplaces, emphasizing the importance of supporting users throughout their journey.

Strategic Acquisitions

Strategic acquisitions played a crucial role in eBay's growth under Whitman's leadership. By acquiring complementary businesses and technologies, eBay could enhance its offerings, enter new markets, and stay ahead of the competition.

- PayPal Acquisition: The acquisition of PayPal in 2002 was a pivotal moment for eBay. PayPal's secure and convenient payment solution addressed a critical need for eBay users and became a major driver of the platform's growth. The success of this acquisition highlighted the importance of identifying and integrating complementary technologies.

- StubHub Acquisition: In 2007, eBay acquired StubHub, a leading ticket resale platform. This acquisition allowed eBay to enter the lucrative event ticketing market and diversify its revenue streams. StubHub's integration with eBay expanded the platform's offerings and demonstrated the value of entering new verticals through strategic acquisitions.

- Gmarket Acquisition: To strengthen its presence in the Asian market, eBay acquired Gmarket, a leading e-commerce platform in South Korea, in 2009. This acquisition provided eBay with a strong foothold in the region and showcased the benefits of acquiring established players to accelerate international expansion.

Innovation and Diversification

Whitman's strategic growth strategy also emphasized innovation and diversification. By exploring new business models and revenue streams, eBay could sustain its growth and remain competitive in a rapidly evolving industry.

- New Revenue Streams: Whitman introduced new revenue streams, such as advertising and promotional opportunities, to diversify eBay's income sources. These initiatives provided additional revenue while enhancing the platform's value proposition for sellers. The success of these strategies highlighted the importance of diversifying revenue streams to ensure long-term sustainability.

- Product Innovation: Whitman encouraged a culture of innovation at eBay, fostering the development of new products and features. Initiatives like eBay Motors, eBay Real Estate, and eBay Stores demonstrated the potential for innovation to drive growth and attract new user segments. This focus on product innovation set a standard for other online marketplaces, emphasizing the importance of continuously evolving to meet user needs.

- Technology Integration: Whitman recognized the importance of integrating cutting-edge technologies to enhance the user experience and streamline operations. The integration of PayPal, for example, provided a seamless payment solution that significantly improved the transaction process. By embracing technology, eBay set a benchmark for other online marketplaces, showcasing the potential for technology to drive growth and improve user satisfaction.

Adaptability: Navigating Challenges and Embracing Change

Meg Whitman's tenure at eBay was marked by her ability to navigate challenges and adapt to a rapidly changing industry. Her adaptability and resilience were crucial for sustaining eBay's growth and maintaining its competitive edge.

Responding to Competitive Pressure

As the e-commerce landscape evolved, eBay faced increasing competition from other online marketplaces and retail giants like Amazon. Whitman's ability to respond to competitive pressure was instrumental in maintaining eBay's market position.

- Innovation and Differentiation: Whitman emphasized the importance of innovation and differentiation to stay ahead of the competition. By introducing new features, enhancing user experience, and exploring new business models, eBay could differentiate itself and maintain its appeal. This focus on innovation highlighted the importance of staying proactive and continuously evolving to meet market demands.

- Strategic Partnerships: Whitman pursued strategic partnerships to enhance eBay's capabilities and expand its reach. Partnerships with companies like Google and Yahoo! helped eBay improve its search functionality and drive traffic to the platform. These collaborations demonstrated the value of leveraging partnerships to enhance competitiveness and drive growth.

- Market Expansion: To mitigate competitive pressure in mature markets, Whitman focused on expanding eBay's presence in emerging markets. By entering new regions and establishing localized marketplaces, eBay could tap into new user bases and diversify its revenue streams. This global expansion strategy showcased the importance of exploring new markets to sustain growth.

Adapting to Technological Advancements

The rapid pace of technological advancements in the e-commerce industry required constant adaptation. Whitman's ability to embrace new technologies and integrate them into eBay's operations was crucial for maintaining the platform's relevance and competitiveness.

- Mobile Commerce: As mobile technology evolved, Whitman recognized the potential for mobile commerce to drive growth. eBay invested in developing mobile apps and optimizing its platform for mobile users, making it easier for buyers and sellers to transact on the go. This focus on mobile commerce set a standard for other online marketplaces, highlighting the importance of embracing mobile technology.

- Data Analytics: Whitman leveraged data analytics to inform strategic decisions and enhance the user experience. By analyzing user behavior, transaction patterns, and market trends, eBay could identify opportunities for improvement and innovation. The use of data-driven insights demonstrated the value of analytics in driving strategic growth and improving user satisfaction.

- Security Enhancements: As online security threats evolved, Whitman prioritized enhancing eBay's security measures to protect users. Investments in advanced security technologies and protocols ensured that eBay could provide a safe and secure marketplace. This commitment to security set a benchmark for other online marketplaces, emphasizing the importance of protecting users in the digital age.

Navigating Regulatory Challenges

eBay's global expansion brought regulatory challenges, including issues related to cross-border trade, taxation, and consumer protection. Whitman's ability to navigate these challenges and ensure compliance was crucial for maintaining eBay's growth and reputation.

- Compliance and Regulation: Whitman worked closely with regulatory authorities and industry stakeholders to address regulatory challenges and ensure compliance with local laws. By fostering positive relationships with regulators, eBay could navigate complex legal environments and maintain its operations. This focus on compliance highlighted the importance of working collaboratively with regulatory bodies.

- Consumer Protection: Whitman prioritized consumer protection, implementing policies and measures to safeguard users. Buyer and seller protection programs, secure payment solutions, and robust dispute resolution mechanisms ensured that users could transact with confidence. These consumer protection initiatives set a standard for other online marketplaces, emphasizing the importance of safeguarding users' interests.

- Cross-Border Trade Facilitation: Whitman championed cross-border trade, implementing measures to facilitate international transactions. This included addressing customs and import/export regulations, providing currency conversion options, and offering international shipping solutions. eBay's success in facilitating cross-border trade demonstrated the value of enabling global commerce and navigating regulatory complexities.

Meg Whitman's leadership at eBay transformed the

company from a fledgling start-up into a global e-commerce giant, setting new standards for the industry and influencing countless other online marketplaces. Her strategic vision, focus on user experience, and ability to navigate challenges and adapt to change were instrumental in eBay's success.

Whitman's impact on the e-commerce industry extends beyond eBay, as her leadership principles and business strategies continue to inspire future generations of business leaders and entrepreneurs. By prioritizing user experience, embracing innovation, and maintaining brand consistency, Whitman demonstrated the potential for online marketplaces to revolutionize the retail industry and create value for users worldwide.

The lessons learned from Whitman's tenure at eBay highlight the importance of strategic growth and adaptability in today's rapidly evolving business landscape. By balancing expansion with core values, leveraging strategic acquisitions, and embracing technological advancements, companies can sustain growth, remain competitive, and make a lasting impact on their industries.

Meg Whitman's legacy at eBay is one of transformation, resilience, and visionary leadership. Her journey serves as an inspiration for those who aspire to lead with purpose, innovate with intention, and navigate the complexities of the modern business world.

Chapter 7: Sara Blakely - The Shapewear Visionary

Sara Blakely's story is a quintessential tale of entrepreneurial ingenuity and perseverance. Born on February 27, 1971, in Clearwater, Florida, Blakely grew up in a family that valued hard work and resilience. Her father was a trial attorney, and her mother was an artist. From a young age, Blakely was encouraged to embrace challenges and learn from failure, a mindset that would become crucial in her entrepreneurial journey.

Blakely attended Florida State University, where she earned a degree in communications. After graduation, she intended to pursue a career in law but failed the LSAT twice. This setback led her to reassess her career path. She moved to Orlando, Florida, and took a job at Walt Disney World, where she worked various roles, including character acting as Goofy. This period, though not glamorous, taught her valuable lessons in dealing with people and maintaining a positive attitude in the face of adversity.

Following her stint at Disney, Blakely worked for seven years as a door-to-door fax machine salesperson for a company called Danka. This job was both challenging and formative; it honed her sales skills and taught her the importance of persistence. Blakely often found herself frustrated by the discomfort of traditional pantyhose, particularly their visible seams and the way they bunched up under white pants. This frustration sparked the idea that would eventually lead to the creation of Spanx.

The Birth of Spanx

In 1998, at the age of 27, Blakely decided to act on her idea to create a new type of undergarment that would be seamless, comfortable, and invisible under clothing. She envisioned a product that would offer the smoothing effects of traditional pantyhose without the discomfort. With no formal background in fashion design or business, Blakely embarked on her entrepreneurial journey with determination and a $5,000 savings she had set aside from her job.

Blakely began by researching fabrics and prototypes, spending countless hours in hosiery mills in North Carolina. Her persistence paid off when she found a mill owner willing to help her develop her idea. With a prototype in hand, Blakely faced the daunting task of bringing her product to market. She quickly learned that the traditional retail landscape was not receptive to new, unproven products, especially from an unknown entrepreneur.

Despite numerous rejections, Blakely remained undeterred. She used her sales skills to secure a meeting with a buyer at Neiman Marcus. In a bold move, she personally demonstrated the product by showing the buyer the difference between wearing traditional pantyhose and Spanx under white pants. This hands-on approach worked, and Neiman Marcus agreed to carry Spanx in their stores.

Blakely's innovative product quickly gained traction. Oprah Winfrey, a highly influential figure in media, featured Spanx on her popular television show, calling it one of her "Favorite Things." This endorsement catapulted Spanx into the national spotlight, driving massive demand and helping Blakely secure additional retail partnerships.

Achievements: Building Spanx into a Multimillion-Dollar Brand

Sara Blakely's journey from a frustrated consumer to a billion-dollar entrepreneur is a testament to her vision, tenacity, and innovative spirit. Her achievements with Spanx have not only revolutionized the shapewear industry but also set new standards for female entrepreneurship.

Revolutionizing Shapewear

Spanx started with a simple but powerful idea: to create a more comfortable and effective shapewear product. Blakely's focus on innovation and quality quickly distinguished Spanx from other undergarments on the market. Unlike traditional pantyhose and shapewear, Spanx products were designed to be seamless, invisible under clothing, and comfortable for extended wear.

Blakely's approach to product development was hands-on and customer-centric. She was involved in every aspect of the process, from selecting fabrics to testing prototypes. This attention to detail ensured that Spanx products met the highest standards of quality and performance. The brand's flagship product, the footless pantyhose, became an instant hit, resonating with women who had long been frustrated by the limitations of traditional undergarments.

Strategic Branding and Marketing

One of the key factors in Spanx's success was Blakely's strategic approach to branding and marketing. She understood the importance of creating a strong, memorable brand that resonated with consumers. The name "Spanx" itself was chosen for its playful and memorable nature, and Blakely's use of humor and authenticity in branding helped distinguish Spanx from its competitors.

Blakely's marketing strategy was innovative and unconventional. Without a large marketing budget, she relied on grassroots efforts and word-of-mouth to generate buzz. She sent samples to fashion editors and influencers, secured product placements in high-profile magazines, and leveraged her own personal story to connect with consumers. This approach not only built brand awareness but also created a loyal customer base.

The turning point for Spanx came when Oprah Winfrey featured the product on her show in 2000. Oprah's endorsement provided an unprecedented level of exposure and credibility, leading to a surge in demand and solidifying Spanx's place in the market. This moment demonstrated the power of strategic influencer partnerships and the importance of timing in marketing.

Expansion and Product Diversification

Under Blakely's leadership, Spanx expanded its product line beyond the original footless pantyhose to include a wide range of shapewear and undergarments. The brand introduced products such as shaping shorts, leggings, bras, and activewear, all designed with the same focus on comfort, quality, and innovation. This diversification allowed Spanx to cater to a broader audience and meet the evolving needs of consumers.

Blakely also recognized the potential for Spanx to enter new markets and demographics. The brand launched Spanx for Men in 2010, offering shapewear and compression garments tailored to male consumers. This move not only expanded the brand's reach but also highlighted Blakely's ability to identify and capitalize on new market opportunities.

Spanx's expansion was not limited to product lines; the brand also expanded its retail presence. Initially available in high-end department stores like Neiman Marcus and Saks Fifth Avenue, Spanx products soon became available in major retailers such as Nordstrom, Target, and Macy's. This broad retail distribution helped make Spanx a household name and accessible to a wider range of consumers.

Building a Billion-Dollar Brand

Sara Blakely's strategic decisions and relentless drive transformed Spanx into a billion-dollar brand. By 2012, just over a decade after its founding, Spanx was valued at over $1 billion, making Blakely the youngest self-made female billionaire at the time. Her success with Spanx earned her numerous accolades and recognition, including being featured on Forbes' list of the World's Most Powerful Women.

Blakely's leadership style and commitment to empowering women have been central to Spanx's success. She fostered a positive and inclusive company culture, emphasizing innovation, collaboration, and a customer-first mindset. Blakely's focus on creating a supportive work environment where employees could thrive helped attract top talent and drive the company's growth.

Philanthropy and Social Impact

In addition to her entrepreneurial achievements, Sara Blakely has made significant contributions to philanthropy and social impact. In 2006, she founded the Sara Blakely Foundation, which focuses on empowering women and girls through education and entrepreneurship. The foundation has funded numerous programs and initiatives aimed at providing women with the resources and opportunities needed to succeed.

Blakely's commitment to giving back extends to her approach to business. She has consistently prioritized corporate social responsibility and ethical practices. Spanx products are designed with sustainability in mind, and the company has implemented initiatives to reduce its environmental impact. Blakely's focus on social and environmental responsibility has set a positive example for other businesses and entrepreneurs.

In 2013, Blakely became the first female billionaire to join the Giving Pledge, a commitment by the world's wealthiest individuals to give the majority of their wealth to charitable causes. Her pledge underscores her dedication to making a positive impact on society and using her success to help others.

Innovation and Future Growth

Sara Blakely's entrepreneurial journey is far from over. She continues to drive innovation and growth at Spanx, exploring new opportunities and markets. Under her leadership, Spanx has embraced technology and digital transformation, enhancing its e-commerce platform and leveraging data analytics to better understand and serve its customers.

Blakely's ability to adapt to changing market dynamics and consumer preferences has been crucial to Spanx's sustained success. She remains actively involved in product development, ensuring that Spanx continues to lead the industry in innovation and quality. This focus on continuous improvement and customer-centricity has positioned Spanx for long-term growth and success.

Looking ahead, Blakely's vision for Spanx includes expanding into new product categories and markets. The brand's commitment to innovation and excellence will continue to drive its growth, and Blakely's entrepreneurial spirit will ensure that Spanx remains at the forefront of the shapewear and apparel industry.

Sara Blakely's remarkable journey from a door-to-door fax machine salesperson to the founder of a billion-dollar shapewear brand is a testament to her vision, determination, and innovative spirit. Her achievements with Spanx have revolutionized the shapewear industry and set new standards for female entrepreneurship.

Blakely's success is built on a foundation of innovation, quality, and a deep understanding of consumer needs. Her strategic approach to branding, marketing, and product development has created a strong and enduring brand that resonates with consumers worldwide. Through her leadership, Blakely has not only built a successful business but also made a positive impact on society through her philanthropy and commitment to empowering women.

Sara Blakely's story is an inspiration to aspiring entrepreneurs and business leaders. Her ability to turn a simple idea into a global brand, her resilience in the face of challenges, and her dedication to giving back demonstrate the power of entrepreneurial ingenuity and the potential for business to drive positive change. As Spanx continues to grow and evolve, Blakely's legacy as a shapewear visionary and trailblazing entrepreneur will undoubtedly endure.

Impact on Industry: Revolutionizing the Shapewear Market and Female Entrepreneurship

When Sara Blakely founded Spanx in 2000, the shapewear market was stagnant and dominated by outdated products that prioritized function over comfort and style. Traditional shapewear often felt like a necessary evil for women seeking a smoother silhouette, but it came with a host of discomforts, including restrictive designs, visible seams, and unflattering fits. Blakely's innovative approach transformed the industry, making shapewear a desirable, comfortable, and empowering choice for women around the world.

Innovative Product Design

One of Blakely's most significant contributions to the shapewear market was her emphasis on innovative product design. Her initial idea for footless pantyhose came from a personal frustration with traditional hosiery, which often bunched up and created visible lines under white pants. This simple yet revolutionary concept laid the foundation for Spanx's success.

- Comfort and Functionality: Blakely's designs prioritized comfort without sacrificing functionality. Spanx products were made from high-quality, breathable materials that provided the desired shaping effect without the discomfort associated with traditional shapewear. The seamless designs and innovative fabric technology allowed for a smooth, invisible fit under clothing.

- Variety and Versatility: Spanx quickly expanded its product line to include a wide range of shapewear items, such as bodysuits, shorts, leggings, bras, and slips. This variety allowed women to choose products that suited their specific needs and preferences. Spanx also introduced different levels of compression, catering to those seeking anything from light shaping to more significant support.

- Style and Confidence: Blakely's designs were not just about shaping the body; they were also about empowering women to feel confident and stylish. Spanx products were available in various colors and styles, making them suitable for everyday wear and special occasions. This focus on aesthetics helped reshape the perception of shapewear from a utilitarian undergarment to a fashion-forward wardrobe staple.

Marketing and Branding

Blakely's approach to marketing and branding was equally innovative. She understood that creating a successful brand required more than just a great product; it required a strong, memorable identity and a deep connection with consumers.

- Memorable Brand Name: The name "Spanx" was chosen for its catchy, playful nature. It stood out in a market dominated by bland, descriptive names and quickly became synonymous with the new wave of shapewear.

The quirky name also made the brand more approachable and relatable, contributing to its rapid growth in popularity.

- Authentic Storytelling: Blakely's personal story of perseverance and innovation resonated with consumers. She often shared her journey from selling fax machines to founding a multimillion-dollar company, highlighting her struggles and triumphs along the way. This authentic storytelling created a strong emotional connection with the brand and inspired countless women to pursue their own entrepreneurial dreams.

- Celebrity Endorsements: One of the most significant boosts to Spanx's visibility came from celebrity endorsements. When Oprah Winfrey featured Spanx on her show as one of her "Favorite Things," the brand received unprecedented exposure and credibility. This endorsement, along with others from high-profile figures in the fashion and entertainment industries, helped Spanx gain mainstream acceptance and become a household name.

Changing Consumer Perceptions

Blakely's impact on the shapewear market extended beyond product innovation and branding; she also played a crucial role in changing consumer perceptions of shapewear.

- Empowerment and Confidence: Spanx's marketing campaigns emphasized empowerment and confidence, positioning shapewear as a tool for women to feel their best. This positive messaging resonated with consumers and helped shift the narrative around shapewear from one of necessity and discomfort to one of choice and empowerment.

- Inclusivity: Spanx has made significant strides in promoting inclusivity within the shapewear market. The brand offers a wide range of sizes to cater to diverse body types and has expanded its product line to include options for different skin tones. This commitment to inclusivity has helped Spanx appeal to a broader audience and set a new standard for the industry.

- Normalizing Shapewear: Blakely's efforts to normalize shapewear as an everyday wardrobe staple have been transformative. By incorporating shapewear into mainstream fashion and promoting it as a confidence-boosting accessory, Spanx has made it more acceptable and even desirable for women to wear shapewear regularly.

Revolutionizing Female Entrepreneurship

Sara Blakely's journey with Spanx is not only a story of product innovation but also a powerful example of female entrepreneurship. Her success has inspired countless women to pursue their own business ventures and has highlighted the unique challenges and opportunities faced by female entrepreneurs.

Breaking Barriers

Blakely's achievements have broken significant barriers for women in business. As one of the few self-made female billionaires, she has demonstrated that women can succeed in male-dominated industries and create impactful, profitable businesses.

- Overcoming Skepticism: Blakely faced considerable skepticism and rejection when she first pitched her idea for Spanx. Many investors and industry professionals doubted the potential of her product and questioned her ability to succeed without formal business experience. Blakely's perseverance in the face of these challenges has served as a powerful example for aspiring female entrepreneurs.

- Self-Funding and Ownership: One of the remarkable aspects of Blakely's journey is her decision to self-fund Spanx with her $5,000 savings. By retaining full ownership of her company, she maintained control over her vision and strategy. This approach allowed her to build the business on her terms and achieve remarkable success without external funding. Blakely's story highlights the importance of self-belief and resourcefulness in entrepreneurship.

- Role Model and Mentor: Blakely has embraced her role as a mentor and advocate for women in business. She regularly shares her experiences and insights through public speaking engagements, interviews, and social media. By being open about her journey and offering practical advice, she has inspired and guided countless women on their entrepreneurial paths.

Advocacy and Philanthropy

Blakely's impact extends beyond her business achievements; she has also been a passionate advocate for women's empowerment and a dedicated philanthropist.

- Sara Blakely Foundation: In 2006, Blakely established the Sara Blakely Foundation, which focuses on empowering women and girls through education and entrepreneurship. The foundation has funded various initiatives, including scholarships, mentorship programs, and support for female entrepreneurs. Blakely's philanthropic efforts reflect her commitment to creating opportunities for women and promoting gender equality.

- The Giving Pledge: In 2013, Blakely became the first female billionaire to join the Giving Pledge, a commitment by the world's wealthiest individuals to give the majority of their wealth to charitable causes. Her pledge underscores her dedication to using her success to make a positive impact on society and support initiatives that empower women and girls.

- Corporate Social Responsibility: Blakely's commitment to social and environmental responsibility is evident in Spanx's corporate practices. The company has implemented sustainability initiatives, such as using eco-friendly materials and reducing waste in its production processes. Blakely's focus on ethical business practices has set a positive example for other companies and highlighted the importance of corporate social responsibility.

Creating a Supportive Ecosystem

Blakely's success has contributed to the development of a more supportive ecosystem for female entrepreneurs. Her story has raised awareness of the unique challenges faced by women in business and has helped drive initiatives aimed at addressing these barriers.

- Access to Capital: One of the key challenges for female entrepreneurs is access to capital. Blakely's self-funding journey has highlighted the need for more funding opportunities and resources for women-led businesses. Her advocacy has contributed to the growth of venture capital firms and funding programs that focus on supporting female entrepreneurs.

- Mentorship and Networking: Blakely's mentorship and networking efforts have helped create a more supportive environment for women in business. By sharing her experiences and connecting with other female entrepreneurs, she has fostered a sense of community and collaboration. This supportive ecosystem is crucial for helping women overcome challenges and achieve success in their ventures.

- Public Awareness and Representation: Blakely's visibility and success have increased public awareness of the contributions and potential of female entrepreneurs. Her story has challenged stereotypes and highlighted the importance of diversity and inclusion in business. By representing women in leadership and entrepreneurship, Blakely has inspired a new generation of female business leaders.

Lessons Learned: Innovation and Persistence

Sara Blakely's journey with Spanx offers valuable lessons in innovation and persistence. Her ability to turn a simple idea into a billion-dollar brand and her unwavering determination in the face of challenges provide powerful insights for entrepreneurs and business leaders.

Innovation: Thinking Outside the Box

Blakely's success with Spanx is rooted in her innovative approach to product design, marketing, and business strategy. Her willingness to think outside the box and challenge the status quo has been a key driver of her achievements.

- Identifying Pain Points: Blakely's innovation began with identifying a common pain point for women—uncomfortable and unflattering shapewear. By focusing on this specific problem and developing a solution that addressed it, she created a product that resonated with consumers and filled a gap in the market.

- Iterative Development: Blakely's approach to product development was iterative and hands-on. She tested multiple prototypes, gathered feedback, and continuously refined her designs to ensure they met the highest standards of quality and comfort. This iterative process allowed her to create a product that truly met the needs of her customers.

- Creative Marketing: Blakely's marketing strategies were innovative and resourceful. Without a large budget, she relied on grassroots efforts, word-of-mouth, and authentic storytelling to build brand awareness. Her use of humor, relatability, and personal connection in branding helped Spanx stand out and connect with consumers on a deeper level.

- Embracing Technology: Blakely's ability to embrace new technologies and integrate them into her business has been crucial for Spanx's growth. From leveraging e-commerce platforms to using data analytics for customer insights, her willingness to adopt and adapt to technological advancements has kept Spanx competitive and relevant.

Persistence: Overcoming Challenges and Staying the Course

Blakely's journey was not without its challenges. Her persistence and resilience in the face of obstacles have been instrumental in her success and offer valuable lessons for aspiring entrepreneurs.

- Handling Rejection: Blakely faced numerous rejections when pitching her idea to investors and retailers. Instead of giving up, she used each rejection as an opportunity to refine her approach and improve her product. Her persistence in the face of rejection highlights the importance of resilience and the ability to learn from setbacks.

- Staying True to Vision: Throughout her journey, Blakely remained true to her vision and values. She believed in her product and its potential to make a difference in women's lives. This unwavering belief helped her navigate challenges and stay focused on her goals, even when the path was difficult.

- Resourcefulness: Blakely's resourcefulness was evident in her ability to self-fund Spanx and find creative solutions to problems. Whether it was cold-calling hosiery mills or personally demonstrating her product to buyers, she used every resource at her disposal to move her business forward. This resourcefulness underscores the importance of being proactive and finding ways to achieve goals, even with limited resources.

- Continuous Learning: Blakely's willingness to

continuously learn and adapt was crucial for her success. She sought feedback, listened to her customers, and remained open to new ideas and improvements. This commitment to continuous learning allowed her to stay ahead of market trends and meet the evolving needs of her customers.

Empowerment and Impact

Blakely's journey is also a testament to the power of empowerment and making a positive impact through business.

- Empowering Women: Blakely's focus on creating products that empower women to feel confident and stylish has had a significant impact on her customers. By prioritizing comfort, quality, and aesthetics, she has helped women embrace shapewear as a positive and empowering choice.

- Giving Back: Blakely's philanthropic efforts and commitment to empowering women through education and entrepreneurship have made a lasting impact. Her work with the Sara Blakely Foundation and other charitable initiatives reflects her dedication to using her success to support and uplift others.

- Inspiring Future Generations: Blakely's story has inspired countless women to pursue their own entrepreneurial dreams and break barriers in business. Her success has challenged stereotypes and highlighted the potential for women to lead and innovate in any industry.

Sara Blakely's remarkable journey from a door-to-door fax machine salesperson to the founder of a billion-dollar shapewear brand is a testament to her vision, determination, and innovative spirit. Her impact on the shapewear market and female entrepreneurship has been profound, setting new standards for product design, marketing, and business strategy.

Blakely's lessons in innovation and persistence provide valuable insights for entrepreneurs and business leaders. Her ability to identify pain points, think outside the box, and stay true to her vision has driven Spanx's success and inspired a new generation of female entrepreneurs. Her focus on empowerment, giving back, and making a positive impact through business underscores the potential for entrepreneurship to drive social change and create lasting value.

As Spanx continues to grow and evolve, Blakely's legacy as a shapewear visionary and trailblazing entrepreneur will undoubtedly endure. Her story serves as an inspiration for those who aspire to lead with purpose, innovate with intention, and navigate the complexities of the modern business world.

Chapter 8: Indra Nooyi - The Corporate Strategist

Indra Nooyi's journey to becoming the CEO of PepsiCo is a story of remarkable determination, strategic acumen, and visionary leadership. Born on October 28, 1955, in Chennai, India, Nooyi grew up in a family that valued education and hard work. Her father was a bank official, and her mother, a homemaker, encouraged her children to think ambitiously about their futures.

Nooyi attended Holy Angels Anglo Indian Higher Secondary School and later graduated from Madras Christian College with a bachelor's degree in Physics, Chemistry, and Mathematics. Her academic prowess and drive for excellence were evident from a young age. After completing her undergraduate studies, she went on to pursue a master's degree in Business Administration from the Indian Institute of Management Calcutta, one of India's premier business schools.

In 1978, Nooyi moved to the United States to further her education at the Yale School of Management, where she earned a Master of Public and Private Management degree. This transition marked the beginning of her ascent in the corporate world. At Yale, Nooyi distinguished herself with her analytical skills and strategic thinking, attributes that would define her career.

Early Career and Corporate Climb

Nooyi's early career included roles at prestigious consulting firms and corporations, where she gained valuable experience in strategy and operations. Her first job in the U.S. was with the Boston Consulting Group (BCG), where she worked on a variety of projects, honing her problem-solving abilities and gaining exposure to different industries.

After BCG, Nooyi took on strategic planning roles at Motorola and Asea Brown Boveri (ABB). At Motorola, she was the vice president and director of corporate strategy and planning, where she played a key role in shaping the company's strategic direction. Her work at ABB involved developing business strategies for the company's industrial and transportation sectors. These experiences broadened her understanding of global business dynamics and reinforced her reputation as a strategic thinker.

Joining PepsiCo

In 1994, Nooyi joined PepsiCo as senior vice president of corporate strategy and development. This move marked the beginning of a long and successful tenure at one of the world's largest food and beverage companies. At PepsiCo, Nooyi's strategic insights and ability to drive change quickly made her a rising star within the organization.

Nooyi's early contributions at PepsiCo included leading the company's restructuring efforts, which aimed to streamline operations and focus on core businesses. Her work in this area helped PepsiCo become more agile and better positioned for growth. She also played a pivotal role in several key acquisitions, including the purchase of Tropicana in 1998, which expanded PepsiCo's portfolio of healthy beverage options.

Rise to Leadership

Nooyi's success in these strategic initiatives led to her promotion to president and chief financial officer (CFO) in 2001. In this role, she oversaw the company's financial operations, strategic planning, and corporate development. Her leadership during this period was marked by a focus on driving growth and improving profitability, while also positioning PepsiCo for long-term success.

In 2006, Nooyi was named CEO of PepsiCo, becoming one of the few women to lead a Fortune 500 company. Her appointment was a testament to her strategic vision, leadership skills, and ability to navigate the complexities of a global corporation. Nooyi's tenure as CEO would be defined by her commitment to growth, sustainability, and innovation.

Achievements: Driving Growth and Sustainability at PepsiCo

Under Indra Nooyi's leadership, PepsiCo achieved significant growth and made substantial strides in sustainability and corporate responsibility. Her tenure as CEO was characterized by bold strategic decisions, a focus on long-term value creation, and a commitment to balancing profitability with social and environmental impact.

Strategic Vision: Performance with Purpose

One of Nooyi's most significant contributions to PepsiCo was the introduction of the "Performance with Purpose" (PwP) strategy. Launched in 2006, PwP was a comprehensive framework that aimed to deliver sustainable growth by integrating social and environmental considerations into the company's business operations.

- Healthy Products Portfolio: Recognizing the growing consumer demand for healthier food and beverage options, Nooyi spearheaded efforts to diversify PepsiCo's product portfolio. The company invested in the development and acquisition of nutritious products, such as Quaker Oats, Naked Juice, and Sabra hummus. This shift towards healthier offerings helped PepsiCo meet evolving consumer preferences and positioned the company as a leader in the health and wellness space.

- Environmental Sustainability: Nooyi's commitment to environmental sustainability was evident in PepsiCo's initiatives to reduce its environmental footprint. The company set ambitious goals to reduce greenhouse gas emissions, conserve water, and minimize waste. Under her leadership, PepsiCo implemented innovative practices, such as water-efficient agriculture and sustainable packaging solutions, to achieve these goals.

- Social Responsibility: Nooyi emphasized the

importance of social responsibility, focusing on improving the lives of communities where PepsiCo operated. The company launched programs to support education, health, and economic development, particularly in underserved regions. These efforts helped build positive relationships with stakeholders and reinforced PepsiCo's reputation as a socially responsible corporation.

Driving Growth Through Innovation and Acquisition

Nooyi's strategic vision extended to driving growth through innovation and strategic acquisitions. Her leadership was marked by a series of bold moves that expanded PepsiCo's capabilities and market reach.

- Innovation in Products and Processes: Nooyi fostered a culture of innovation at PepsiCo, encouraging teams to develop new products and improve existing ones. The company invested in research and development (R&D) to create cutting-edge products that met changing consumer preferences. This focus on innovation led to the launch of successful products, such as PepsiCo's line of zero-calorie beverages and new snack offerings.

- Strategic Acquisitions: Nooyi's strategic acumen was evident in her approach to acquisitions. She identified opportunities to acquire companies that complemented PepsiCo's core businesses and enhanced its product portfolio. Notable acquisitions during her tenure included the purchase of Tropicana, Quaker Oats, and Wimm-Bill-Dann, a leading dairy company in Russia. These acquisitions not only expanded PepsiCo's product offerings but also strengthened its presence in key markets.

- Global Expansion: Under Nooyi's leadership, PepsiCo expanded its global footprint, entering new markets and strengthening its position in existing ones. The company focused on high-growth regions, such as Asia, Africa, and Latin America, to capitalize on emerging market opportunities. This global expansion strategy helped PepsiCo achieve sustained growth and diversify its revenue streams.

Financial Performance and Shareholder Value

Nooyi's tenure as CEO was marked by strong financial performance and value creation for shareholders. Her strategic initiatives and focus on operational efficiency drove significant growth and profitability.

- Revenue and Profit Growth: Under Nooyi's leadership, PepsiCo's revenue grew from $35 billion in 2006 to $63.5 billion in 2017. This impressive growth was driven by a combination of product innovation, strategic acquisitions, and global expansion. The company's profitability also improved, with net income increasing significantly during her tenure.

- Shareholder Returns: Nooyi's commitment to

delivering value for shareholders was evident in PepsiCo's strong stock performance. The company's stock price more than doubled during her tenure, reflecting investor confidence in her strategic vision and leadership. PepsiCo also consistently returned value to shareholders through dividends and share buybacks.

- Operational Efficiency: Nooyi implemented initiatives to improve operational efficiency and reduce costs. The company invested in technology and process improvements to streamline operations and enhance productivity. These efforts helped PepsiCo achieve significant cost savings and improve its competitive position.

Leadership and Corporate Culture

Nooyi's impact on PepsiCo extended beyond financial performance; she also played a crucial role in shaping the company's leadership and corporate culture.

- Inclusive Leadership: Nooyi was a strong advocate for diversity and inclusion, both within PepsiCo and in the broader business community. She championed initiatives to increase the representation of women and minorities in leadership positions and fostered an inclusive workplace culture. Her efforts helped create a more diverse and dynamic leadership team at PepsiCo.

- Employee Engagement: Nooyi believed in the

importance of engaging and empowering employees. She implemented programs to support employee development, well-being, and work-life balance. These initiatives contributed to high levels of employee satisfaction and retention, reinforcing PepsiCo's reputation as an employer of choice.

- Ethical Governance: Nooyi emphasized the importance of ethical governance and corporate responsibility. She instilled a culture of integrity and accountability, ensuring that PepsiCo operated in accordance with the highest ethical standards. This commitment to ethical governance helped build trust with stakeholders and protect the company's reputation.

Legacy and Impact

Indra Nooyi's tenure as CEO of PepsiCo left a lasting legacy, both for the company and for the broader business community. Her visionary leadership, strategic acumen, and commitment to sustainability and social responsibility have had a profound impact on PepsiCo and the industry as a whole.

- Transformation and Growth: Nooyi's strategic initiatives transformed PepsiCo into a more agile, innovative, and sustainable company. Her focus on long-term value creation and responsible growth positioned PepsiCo for continued success in an evolving market landscape.

- Role Model and Trailblazer: Nooyi's achievements as a female CEO in a male-dominated industry have made her a role model and trailblazer for women in business. Her success has inspired countless women to pursue leadership roles and break barriers in their careers.

- Sustainability and Responsibility: Nooyi's legacy includes her commitment to sustainability and corporate responsibility. Her "Performance with Purpose" strategy set a new standard for integrating social and environmental considerations into business operations. This approach has influenced other companies to adopt more sustainable and responsible practices.

Lessons Learned: Innovation and Persistence

Indra Nooyi's journey and achievements offer valuable lessons in innovation and persistence. Her ability to drive transformative change at PepsiCo and her unwavering commitment to her strategic vision provide powerful insights for leaders and entrepreneurs.

Innovation: Embracing Change and Driving Progress

Nooyi's success at PepsiCo was rooted in her ability to embrace change and drive innovation. Her approach to innovation was comprehensive, encompassing product development, business processes, and corporate strategy.

- Proactive Change Management: Nooyi understood the importance of proactively managing change in a rapidly evolving business environment. She was not afraid to make bold decisions and implement transformative initiatives to position PepsiCo for long-term success. Her willingness to embrace change and take calculated risks was a key driver of innovation at the company.

- Customer-Centric Innovation: Nooyi's focus on customer needs and preferences was central to her innovation strategy. She recognized that consumer expectations were shifting towards healthier and more sustainable products. By aligning PepsiCo's product development with these trends, she ensured that the company remained relevant and competitive.

- Collaborative Innovation: Nooyi fostered a culture of collaboration and cross-functional innovation at PepsiCo. She encouraged teams to work together, share ideas, and leverage diverse perspectives to drive creativity and problem-solving. This collaborative approach enabled PepsiCo to develop innovative products and solutions that met the needs of a diverse and global customer base.

- Investment in R&D: Nooyi's commitment to innovation was reflected in her significant investments in research and development (R&D). She recognized that continuous investment in R&D was essential for staying ahead of market trends and technological advancements. PepsiCo's R&D efforts under her leadership led to the development of breakthrough products and processes that drove growth and differentiation.

Persistence: Overcoming Challenges and Staying the Course

Nooyi's journey was marked by her persistence and resilience in the face of challenges. Her ability to stay focused on her vision and navigate obstacles provides valuable lessons for leaders and entrepreneurs.

- Navigating Industry Challenges: The food and beverage industry faced numerous challenges during Nooyi's tenure, including changing consumer preferences, regulatory pressures, and competitive dynamics. Nooyi's persistence in addressing these challenges and finding innovative solutions was crucial for PepsiCo's success. Her ability to adapt to industry shifts and stay ahead of the curve demonstrated her resilience and strategic foresight.

- Maintaining Long-Term Focus: Nooyi's strategic vision for PepsiCo was centered on long-term value creation. She remained focused on her goals, even when faced with short-term pressures and setbacks. Her persistence in pursuing sustainable growth and responsible business practices underscored her commitment to creating lasting impact and value for stakeholders.

- Building a Resilient Organization: Nooyi's leadership was characterized by her efforts to build a resilient organization that could withstand external shocks and adapt to changing market conditions. She implemented initiatives to enhance operational efficiency, strengthen supply chains, and foster a culture of agility and innovation. These efforts helped PepsiCo navigate economic downturns, market disruptions, and other challenges with resilience and strength.

- Personal Resilience: Nooyi's personal resilience and determination were evident throughout her career. As an immigrant and woman of color in a male-dominated industry, she faced unique challenges and biases. Her ability to overcome these barriers and rise to the top of a global corporation is a testament to her perseverance and inner strength. Nooyi's story serves as an inspiration for individuals facing adversity and striving to achieve their goals.

Leadership and Vision

Nooyi's leadership style and strategic vision were instrumental in her success at PepsiCo. Her approach to leadership offers valuable lessons for current and aspiring leaders.

- Visionary Leadership: Nooyi's ability to articulate a clear and compelling vision for PepsiCo was a key factor in her success. Her "Performance with Purpose" strategy provided a roadmap for the company's growth and sustainability efforts. By aligning the organization around a shared vision, she inspired and mobilized teams to achieve ambitious goals.

- Inclusive Leadership: Nooyi's commitment to diversity and inclusion was central to her leadership philosophy. She believed that diverse perspectives and experiences were critical for driving innovation and achieving business success. Her efforts to promote inclusivity and representation within PepsiCo created a more dynamic and high-performing organization.

- Empathetic Leadership: Nooyi's empathetic leadership style set her apart as a leader who genuinely cared about her employees and stakeholders. She prioritized employee well-being, work-life balance, and development, fostering a supportive and positive work environment. Her empathetic approach built trust and loyalty within the organization and contributed to PepsiCo's strong corporate culture.

- Strategic Decision-Making: Nooyi's strategic acumen was evident in her ability to make bold and informed decisions. She leveraged data, insights, and stakeholder input to guide her decision-making process. Her strategic choices, from acquisitions to sustainability initiatives, were grounded in a deep understanding of market dynamics and long-term trends.

Impact and Legacy

Indra Nooyi's impact on PepsiCo and the broader business community extends beyond her tenure as CEO. Her legacy includes significant contributions to corporate strategy, sustainability, and leadership.

- Transformational Impact: Nooyi's strategic initiatives transformed PepsiCo into a more sustainable, innovative, and globally competitive company. Her focus on long-term value creation and responsible growth positioned PepsiCo for continued success and set new standards for the industry.

- Influence on Sustainability: Nooyi's "Performance with Purpose" strategy has had a lasting impact on corporate sustainability. Her efforts to integrate social and environmental considerations into business operations have influenced other companies to adopt more sustainable practices. Her legacy includes a commitment to creating positive social and environmental impact through business.

- Inspiration for Women Leaders: Nooyi's achievements as a female CEO in a male-dominated industry have made her a role model for women in business. Her success has inspired countless women to pursue leadership roles and break barriers in their careers. Nooyi's advocacy for diversity and inclusion has contributed to greater representation and empowerment of women in the corporate world.

- Philanthropic Impact: Nooyi's philanthropic efforts, including her support for education, health, and economic development, reflect her commitment to giving back and making a positive impact on society. Her contributions to social causes and community development have created lasting benefits for individuals and communities.

Indra Nooyi's journey from Chennai, India, to the CEO of PepsiCo is a story of visionary leadership, strategic acumen, and unwavering determination. Her impact on the food and beverage industry, corporate sustainability, and female entrepreneurship is profound and far-reaching.

Under Nooyi's leadership, PepsiCo achieved significant growth, innovation, and sustainability. Her "Performance with Purpose" strategy set new standards for integrating social and environmental considerations into business operations. Nooyi's strategic initiatives, from product innovation to global expansion, drove significant value creation for shareholders and stakeholders.

Nooyi's lessons in innovation and persistence provide valuable insights for leaders and entrepreneurs. Her ability to embrace change, drive innovation, and navigate challenges with resilience underscores the importance of strategic vision and adaptability in achieving success.

Indra Nooyi's legacy includes her contributions to corporate strategy, sustainability, and leadership. Her impact as a trailblazing female CEO and advocate for diversity and inclusion has inspired a new generation of women leaders. As a visionary and transformative leader, Nooyi's story serves as a powerful example of the potential for business to drive positive change and create lasting impact.

Impact on Industry: Advocating for Corporate Responsibility and Health

Indra Nooyi's tenure as CEO of PepsiCo is often highlighted for her strategic vision and relentless pursuit of corporate responsibility. She understood that long-term business success is inextricably linked to the well-being of society and the environment. Her comprehensive "Performance with Purpose" (PwP) strategy aimed to align PepsiCo's financial performance with its responsibility to the planet and its people.

Environmental Sustainability Initiatives

Nooyi prioritized environmental sustainability, recognizing the importance of reducing PepsiCo's ecological footprint. Under her leadership, the company implemented numerous initiatives to address climate change, water scarcity, and waste reduction.

- Climate Action: PepsiCo committed to reducing greenhouse gas emissions across its value chain. This involved optimizing manufacturing processes, investing in energy-efficient technologies, and transitioning to renewable energy sources. The company set ambitious targets for reducing emissions, which included specific goals for its direct operations as well as its supply chain.

- Water Stewardship: Nooyi recognized that water scarcity posed a significant risk to global communities and PepsiCo's business operations. The company launched initiatives to improve water efficiency, particularly in water-stressed regions. PepsiCo worked on replenishing water through various watershed conservation projects, ensuring that the water used in their products was responsibly managed.

- Waste Reduction and Circular Economy: Nooyi championed the reduction of plastic waste and the transition to a circular economy. PepsiCo committed to designing all its packaging to be recyclable, compostable, or biodegradable. The company also invested in developing sustainable packaging solutions, such as the use of plant-based materials and the implementation of recycling programs.

Nutritional Improvements and Health Initiatives

Understanding the shifting consumer preferences towards healthier options, Nooyi drove PepsiCo to reformulate its product portfolio to include more nutritious offerings. This was part of her broader strategy to align the company's operations with public health goals.

- Product Reformulation: Under Nooyi's leadership, PepsiCo undertook significant efforts to reduce the levels of sugar, sodium, and saturated fats in its products. This involved extensive research and development to create healthier alternatives without compromising on taste. Products like Pepsi Zero Sugar and reduced-fat Lay's potato chips emerged from these reformulation efforts.

- Expansion of Healthier Products: Nooyi led PepsiCo's strategic acquisitions of health-oriented brands such as Tropicana, Quaker Oats, and Naked Juice. These acquisitions diversified PepsiCo's product portfolio and positioned the company as a leader in the health and wellness sector. The company also launched new products under existing brands, like organic Gatorade and gluten-free snacks, to cater to health-conscious consumers.

- Transparency and Labeling: PepsiCo under Nooyi also committed to transparency in its nutritional information. The company enhanced its product labeling to provide clear and accessible information about nutritional content. This move was aimed at helping consumers make informed choices and fostering trust in the brand.

Social Responsibility and Community Engagement

Nooyi's vision of corporate responsibility extended beyond environmental and health concerns. She believed in PepsiCo's role in supporting communities and fostering social equity.

- Community Development: PepsiCo invested in various community development programs, focusing on education, health, and economic empowerment. These initiatives aimed to improve the quality of life in the communities where the company operated. For instance, PepsiCo supported educational programs in underserved areas and provided resources to promote local entrepreneurship.

- Employee Well-Being: Recognizing that employees are a company's greatest asset, Nooyi implemented programs to support their well-being and professional growth. PepsiCo offered comprehensive health and wellness programs, flexible work arrangements, and opportunities for skill development. This focus on employee welfare helped build a positive and inclusive workplace culture.

- Diversity and Inclusion: Nooyi was a strong advocate for diversity and inclusion. Under her leadership, PepsiCo launched initiatives to increase the representation of women and minorities at all levels of the organization. The company implemented unconscious bias training, mentorship programs, and policies to ensure equal opportunities for all employees. These efforts not only enhanced the company's culture but also contributed to its innovative capacity by bringing diverse perspectives to the table.

Impact on Industry Standards

Indra Nooyi's commitment to corporate responsibility and health set new standards for the industry. Her initiatives demonstrated that it is possible to achieve business success while making a positive impact on society and the environment.

- Inspiration for Other Companies: Nooyi's approach inspired other companies to adopt similar sustainability and health initiatives. Her emphasis on integrating corporate responsibility into the core business strategy showed that such efforts could drive long-term growth and resilience. Companies across various industries began to recognize the importance of aligning their operations with broader social and environmental goals.

- Industry Collaboration: Nooyi also played a role in fostering collaboration within the industry to address common challenges. PepsiCo participated in various industry coalitions and initiatives aimed at promoting sustainability and public health. This collaborative approach helped accelerate progress on key issues and demonstrated the power of collective action.

- Consumer Expectations: Nooyi's leadership helped shift consumer expectations regarding corporate responsibility. Consumers began to demand more from companies, expecting them to take active roles in addressing social and environmental issues. This shift in consumer behavior pushed companies to adopt more sustainable and responsible practices to remain competitive.

Lessons Learned: Strategic Vision and Sustainable Leadership

Indra Nooyi's leadership at PepsiCo provides valuable lessons in strategic vision and sustainable leadership. Her ability to drive transformative change while maintaining a focus on long-term value creation offers insights for leaders and organizations aiming to navigate complex and dynamic environments.

Strategic Vision: Setting a Long-Term Agenda

Nooyi's strategic vision was characterized by her ability to set a long-term agenda that balanced immediate business needs with future sustainability.

- Holistic Approach: Nooyi's "Performance with Purpose" strategy was a holistic approach that integrated financial performance with social and environmental responsibility. This comprehensive framework ensured that all aspects of the business were aligned with the company's broader mission and values. Leaders can learn from this approach by adopting strategies that consider multiple dimensions of success and drive holistic growth.

- Clear and Compelling Vision: Nooyi was able to articulate a clear and compelling vision for

PepsiCo's future. Her ability to communicate this vision effectively inspired and mobilized employees, stakeholders, and partners. A clear vision serves as a guiding star for the organization, providing direction and motivation, especially during times of change and uncertainty.

- Focus on Innovation: Nooyi's strategic vision included a strong focus on innovation. She understood that staying ahead of market trends and technological advancements was crucial for maintaining a competitive edge. Leaders should prioritize innovation and invest in research and development to drive continuous improvement and differentiation.

- Alignment with Global Trends: Nooyi aligned PepsiCo's strategy with global trends such as health and wellness, sustainability, and social responsibility. By addressing these macro trends, she ensured that the company remained relevant and resilient in a rapidly changing world. Leaders can benefit from staying attuned to global trends and adapting their strategies accordingly.

Sustainable Leadership: Balancing Profit with Purpose

Nooyi's leadership exemplified the principles of sustainable leadership, which involves balancing profit with purpose and considering the long-term impact of business decisions.

- Ethical Decision-Making: Nooyi's commitment to ethical decision-making was a cornerstone of her leadership. She believed in doing the right thing for the right reasons, even if it meant making difficult choices. Leaders should prioritize ethics and integrity in their decision-making processes to build trust and credibility with stakeholders.

- Stakeholder Engagement: Nooyi understood the importance of engaging with a wide range of stakeholders, including employees, customers, investors, and communities. She fostered open communication and collaboration, ensuring that stakeholder perspectives were considered in strategic decisions. Effective stakeholder engagement helps build strong relationships and enhances the company's social license to operate.

- Resilience and Adaptability: Nooyi demonstrated resilience and adaptability in navigating challenges and uncertainties. Her ability to pivot and adapt to changing market conditions was crucial for PepsiCo's success. Leaders should cultivate resilience and flexibility, enabling their organizations to respond effectively to disruptions and capitalize on new opportunities.

- Long-Term Thinking: Nooyi's focus on long-term thinking was evident in her sustainability initiatives and strategic investments. She prioritized actions that would create lasting value for the company and society. Leaders should adopt a long-term perspective, making decisions that balance short-term gains with future sustainability.

Driving Organizational Change

One of Nooyi's most significant achievements was her ability to drive organizational change and transform PepsiCo into a more sustainable and responsible company.

- Culture of Sustainability: Nooyi embedded sustainability into PepsiCo's corporate culture. She ensured that sustainability goals were integrated into performance metrics and incentives, aligning employee efforts with the company's mission. Building a culture of sustainability requires consistent communication, leadership commitment, and the integration of sustainability into everyday business practices.

- Cross-Functional Collaboration: Nooyi fostered cross-functional collaboration to drive sustainability initiatives. She encouraged teams from different departments to work together, leveraging their diverse expertise to develop innovative solutions. Cross-functional collaboration enhances creativity and problem-solving, enabling organizations to address complex challenges effectively.

- Capacity Building: Nooyi invested in building the capacity of employees to support sustainability efforts. This included training programs, leadership development, and the provision of resources and tools. Empowering employees with the knowledge and skills to contribute to sustainability goals strengthens the organization's ability to achieve its mission.

- Transparency and Accountability: Nooyi emphasized transparency and accountability in reporting progress towards sustainability goals. PepsiCo published regular sustainability reports, providing stakeholders with updates on achievements and challenges. Transparent reporting builds trust and demonstrates the company's commitment to accountability and continuous improvement.

Creating Shared Value

Nooyi's leadership demonstrated the concept of creating shared value, where business success is linked to social and environmental impact.

- Alignment of Business and Social Goals: Nooyi aligned PepsiCo's business goals with social and environmental objectives. By addressing societal challenges such as health and sustainability, she created value for both the company and the broader community. Leaders should seek opportunities to align their business strategies with societal needs, creating mutually beneficial outcomes.

- Partnerships for Impact: Nooyi recognized the importance of partnerships in achieving sustainability goals. She collaborated with governments, non-profits, and other companies to leverage resources and expertise. Partnerships amplify impact and enable organizations to address complex challenges more effectively.

- Measuring Impact: Nooyi emphasized the importance of measuring the impact of sustainability initiatives. PepsiCo developed metrics to track progress and assess the effectiveness of its programs. Measuring impact helps organizations understand the value of their efforts and identify areas for improvement.

- Communicating Success: Nooyi effectively communicated the success and impact of PepsiCo's sustainability initiatives to stakeholders. This helped build a positive reputation for the company and demonstrated the business case for sustainability. Leaders should prioritize clear and consistent communication to share their organization's achievements and inspire others to take action.

Indra Nooyi's leadership at PepsiCo is a powerful example of how strategic vision and sustainable leadership can drive transformative change in a global corporation. Her commitment to corporate responsibility and health set new standards for the industry and demonstrated the potential for business to create positive social and environmental impact.

Nooyi's strategic vision, encapsulated in the "Performance with Purpose" strategy, provided a comprehensive framework for aligning financial performance with sustainability goals. Her focus on innovation, ethical decision-making, and stakeholder engagement helped PepsiCo navigate complex challenges and achieve long-term success.

The lessons learned from Nooyi's tenure at PepsiCo offer valuable insights for leaders and organizations aiming to balance profit with purpose. By embracing change, fostering a culture of sustainability, and creating shared value, leaders can drive growth while contributing to the well-being of society and the planet.

Indra Nooyi's legacy extends beyond her achievements at PepsiCo. Her impact as a trailblazing female CEO, advocate for diversity and inclusion, and champion of corporate responsibility has inspired a new generation of leaders to pursue sustainable and ethical business practices. Her story serves as a testament to the power of visionary leadership and the potential for business to be a force for good in the world.

Chapter 9: Angela Ahrendts - The Luxury Retail Leader

Angela Ahrendts was born on June 7, 1960, in New Palestine, Indiana. She grew up in a close-knit family, the third of six children. Her father was a businessman, and her mother was a homemaker who nurtured creativity and a strong work ethic in their children. From a young age, Ahrendts demonstrated a keen interest in fashion and design, often creating her own clothes and accessories.

Ahrendts attended Ball State University, where she majored in Merchandising and Marketing. After graduating in 1981, she moved to New York City to pursue her passion for fashion. Her early career included roles at various fashion companies, where she gained valuable experience and honed her skills in merchandising, marketing, and brand management.

Early Career in Fashion

Ahrendts' first significant role was at Donna Karan International, where she worked as a Merchandising Manager. Her talent and dedication quickly earned her a promotion to Vice President of Merchandising and Marketing. During her time at Donna Karan, Ahrendts played a crucial role in expanding the brand's presence and establishing its reputation for luxury and innovation.

In 1996, Ahrendts joined Henri Bendel, a prestigious specialty store in New York, as Vice President of

Merchandising and Design. Her work at Henri Bendel further solidified her reputation as a visionary leader in the fashion industry. Ahrendts then moved to Fifth & Pacific Companies (formerly known as Liz Claiborne Inc.), where she served as Executive Vice President. In this role, she was responsible for overseeing multiple brands and driving growth through strategic marketing and merchandising initiatives.

Transition to Burberry

In 2006, Angela Ahrendts took on one of the most significant challenges of her career when she was appointed CEO of Burberry. At the time, Burberry was struggling with brand dilution and declining relevance. Ahrendts was tasked with revitalizing the iconic British brand and restoring its status as a leader in luxury fashion.

Ahrendts' appointment marked the beginning of a transformative period for Burberry. She brought a fresh perspective to the company, combining her deep understanding of fashion with innovative business strategies. Her vision for Burberry centered on leveraging the brand's rich heritage while embracing modern technology and digital marketing.

Achievements: Transforming Burberry and Leading Apple's Retail Strategy

Angela Ahrendts' tenure at Burberry is often cited as one of the most successful brand turnarounds in the fashion industry. Her strategic initiatives and leadership transformed Burberry from a struggling heritage brand into a modern, digitally-savvy luxury powerhouse.

Rebranding and Revitalization

One of Ahrendts' first initiatives at Burberry was to revitalize the brand's image. She worked closely with Chief Creative Officer Christopher Bailey to redefine Burberry's identity and ensure consistency across all touchpoints. Together, they developed a cohesive brand strategy that celebrated Burberry's heritage while incorporating contemporary elements.

- Focus on Heritage: Ahrendts and Bailey emphasized Burberry's British heritage, leveraging iconic symbols such as the trench coat and the check pattern. They ensured that these elements were prominently featured in marketing campaigns and product designs, reinforcing the brand's identity and authenticity.

- Modernizing Product Lines: Ahrendts introduced new product lines and updated existing ones to appeal to a younger, fashion-forward audience. This included launching the Burberry Prorsum line, which showcased innovative and avant-garde designs, and expanding the brand's accessories and beauty offerings.

- Consistent Brand Messaging: Ahrendts ensured that Burberry's messaging was consistent across all channels, from advertising and social media to in-store experiences. This consistency helped build a strong, recognizable brand identity and increased customer loyalty.

Digital Innovation

Ahrendts was a pioneer in integrating digital technology into the luxury retail experience. Under her leadership, Burberry became known for its innovative use of technology to engage with customers and enhance the shopping experience.

- E-Commerce Expansion: Ahrendts prioritized the development of Burberry's e-commerce platform, recognizing the growing importance of online shopping. The company's website was redesigned to offer a seamless, user-friendly experience, and Burberry invested in digital marketing to drive online sales.

- Social Media Engagement: Burberry was one of the first luxury brands to embrace social media as a key marketing tool. Ahrendts oversaw the launch of Burberry's social media accounts and encouraged active engagement with customers. The brand's innovative use of platforms like Instagram, Twitter, and Facebook helped it connect with a global audience and build a strong online community.

- In-Store Technology: Ahrendts introduced cutting-edge technology in Burberry's flagship stores to create a more immersive shopping experience. This included installing large digital screens to display live-streamed runway shows and implementing RFID technology to provide customers with detailed product information. These innovations blurred the lines between physical and digital retail, setting new standards for the industry.

Financial Performance

Ahrendts' strategic initiatives had a significant impact on Burberry's financial performance. Under her leadership, the company experienced substantial growth in revenue and profitability.

- Revenue Growth: During Ahrendts' tenure, Burberry's revenue more than doubled, from approximately £1 billion in 2006 to over £2 billion in 2014. This impressive growth was driven by increased sales in both established and emerging markets, as well as the successful expansion of Burberry's product lines.

- Global Expansion: Ahrendts focused on expanding Burberry's presence in key international markets, including China, the Middle East, and the United States. The company opened new flagship stores in major cities and increased its marketing efforts to attract a global customer base. This international expansion was instrumental in driving Burberry's revenue growth.

- Stock Performance: Burberry's stock price reflected the company's strong performance under Ahrendts' leadership. The stock price increased significantly, providing substantial returns for shareholders and reinforcing investor confidence in the company's strategic direction.

Sustainability and Corporate Responsibility

Ahrendts also prioritized sustainability and corporate responsibility during her time at Burberry. She recognized that these initiatives were essential for long-term success and brand reputation.

- Sustainable Practices: Burberry implemented various initiatives to reduce its environmental impact, including sustainable sourcing of materials, waste reduction, and energy efficiency programs. The company also launched a program to upcycle leftover fabric into new products, promoting a circular economy.

- Community Engagement: Ahrendts encouraged Burberry to engage with local communities and support charitable causes. The company partnered with organizations to promote education, arts, and social welfare, reinforcing its commitment to making a positive impact on society.

- Ethical Supply Chain: Under Ahrendts' leadership, Burberry focused on ensuring that its supply chain adhered to high ethical standards. This included implementing strict labor practices, promoting fair wages, and ensuring safe working conditions for all employees.

Leading Apple's Retail Strategy

In 2014, Angela Ahrendts made a significant career move by joining Apple as Senior Vice President of Retail and Online Stores. Her appointment was a testament to her success at Burberry and her ability to blend fashion and technology. At Apple, Ahrendts was tasked with overseeing the company's global retail operations and enhancing the customer experience across both physical and digital channels.

Transforming Apple Retail

Ahrendts' leadership at Apple was marked by her efforts to transform the company's retail strategy and create a more immersive, community-focused shopping experience.

- Redesigning Apple Stores: One of Ahrendts' first initiatives was to redesign Apple's flagship stores to make them more inviting and community-oriented. The new store designs featured open layouts, natural light, and communal spaces for customers to gather and interact. These changes aimed to create a more welcoming and engaging environment, enhancing the overall customer experience.

- Introducing "Today at Apple": Ahrendts launched the "Today at Apple" program, which offered free educational sessions and workshops in Apple stores. These sessions covered a wide range of topics, from photography and music to coding and app development. The program aimed to empower customers with new skills and foster a sense of community within Apple stores.

- Expanding Retail Presence: Ahrendts oversaw the expansion of Apple's retail presence, opening new stores in key international markets and renovating existing ones. She focused on creating flagship stores in iconic locations, such as the Apple Store in Milan's Piazza Liberty and the Apple Store in Dubai Mall. These flagship stores showcased Apple's commitment to design excellence and provided unique experiences for customers.

Enhancing Customer Experience

Ahrendts' customer-centric approach was central to her strategy at Apple. She believed that creating memorable experiences for customers was essential for building brand loyalty and driving sales.

- Personalized Service: Ahrendts emphasized the importance of personalized service in Apple stores. She introduced new training programs for employees, known as "Creative Pros" and "Technical Experts," to ensure they could provide expert advice and support to customers. This focus on personalized service helped create a more engaging and satisfying shopping experience.

- Seamless Integration of Online and Offline Channels: Ahrendts worked to seamlessly integrate Apple's online and offline retail channels, providing customers with a consistent and cohesive experience. This included enhancements to the Apple website and app, as well as new services like "Buy Online, Pick Up In Store" and same-day delivery. By bridging the gap between digital and physical retail, Ahrendts ensured that customers could interact with Apple in the way that best suited their needs.

- Focus on Community: Ahrendts aimed to make Apple stores more than just places to buy products; she wanted them to be centers of creativity and learning. The "Today at Apple" sessions and community events created opportunities for customers to connect, learn, and share their passions. This community-focused approach helped strengthen the bond between Apple and its customers.

Financial Performance and Growth

Ahrendts' strategic initiatives had a positive impact on Apple's retail performance, contributing to the company's overall growth and success.

- Increased Revenue: During Ahrendts' tenure, Apple's retail division experienced significant revenue growth. The company's focus on enhancing the customer experience and expanding its retail presence helped drive higher sales both in-store and online.

- Improved Customer Satisfaction: Ahrendts' efforts to create a more engaging and personalized shopping experience led to improved customer satisfaction. Apple consistently ranked high in customer satisfaction surveys, reflecting the success of her initiatives.

- Expansion in Key Markets: Ahrendts played a key role in expanding Apple's presence in important international markets, particularly in Asia and the Middle East. The new flagship stores in these regions not only boosted sales but also reinforced Apple's brand image as a leader in innovation and design.

Leadership and Corporate Culture

Ahrendts' leadership style and focus on corporate culture were instrumental in her success at both Burberry and Apple.

- People-Centric Leadership: Ahrendts was known for her people-centric leadership style. She believed in the importance of empowering employees and creating a positive work environment. At both Burberry and Apple, she implemented programs to support employee development, well-being, and engagement. This focus on people helped build strong, motivated teams that were committed to the company's success.

- Inclusive Leadership: Ahrendts was a strong advocate for diversity and inclusion. She promoted initiatives to increase the representation of women and minorities in leadership roles and fostered an inclusive workplace culture. Her efforts to promote diversity and inclusion helped create a more dynamic and innovative organization.

- Visionary Leadership: Ahrendts was a visionary leader who could articulate a clear and compelling vision for the future. Her ability to inspire and mobilize teams around a shared vision was a key factor in her success. Whether at Burberry or Apple, Ahrendts' visionary leadership helped drive transformative change and achieve ambitious goals.

Legacy and Impact

Angela Ahrendts' legacy as a leader in luxury retail and technology is marked by her transformative impact on both Burberry and Apple. Her strategic initiatives, focus on innovation, and commitment to creating positive customer experiences have left a lasting mark on both industries.

- Transformational Leadership: Ahrendts' ability to transform struggling brands into industry leaders is a testament to her strategic vision and leadership skills. Her success at Burberry and Apple demonstrates the power of combining traditional brand values with modern technology and innovation.

- Advancing Digital Retail: Ahrendts was a pioneer in integrating digital technology into the retail experience. Her innovative use of e-commerce, social media, and in-store technology set new standards for the industry and paved the way for the future of retail.

- Championing Customer Experience: Ahrendts' customer-centric approach has had a lasting impact on how brands interact with their customers. Her emphasis on creating memorable and engaging experiences has influenced retail strategies across various industries.

- Inspiring Women Leaders: As a successful female leader in male-dominated industries, Ahrendts has inspired countless women to pursue leadership roles and break barriers in their careers. Her achievements serve as a powerful example of what is possible with vision, determination, and a commitment to excellence.

Angela Ahrendts' career is a remarkable journey of transformation, innovation, and leadership. Her ability to turn around Burberry and lead Apple's retail strategy highlights her strategic vision and commitment to excellence. Ahrendts' impact on the fashion and technology industries is profound, and her legacy as a luxury retail leader continues to inspire and influence the future of retail.

Through her work at Burberry, Ahrendts demonstrated the power of revitalizing a heritage brand by embracing its roots while integrating modern elements. Her success in leveraging digital technology and creating consistent, compelling brand experiences set new benchmarks for the fashion industry.

At Apple, Ahrendts redefined the retail experience, making it more personalized, community-focused, and seamlessly integrated with digital channels. Her initiatives enhanced customer satisfaction and drove significant growth for Apple's retail division.

Angela Ahrendts' story is a testament to the impact of visionary leadership and strategic innovation. Her journey offers valuable lessons for leaders and organizations aiming to navigate the complexities of modern business and create lasting value for customers, employees, and stakeholders.

Impact on Industry: Bridging Luxury Retail with Digital Innovation

Angela Ahrendts' impact on the luxury retail industry is profound, particularly in her strategic integration of digital innovation with traditional luxury retail practices. Her tenure at Burberry is often cited as a paradigm shift in the fashion industry, setting new standards for how luxury brands can leverage technology to enhance their brand presence, customer engagement, and operational efficiency.

Embracing Digital Transformation

When Ahrendts joined Burberry in 2006, she faced the challenge of revitalizing a brand that had lost its way. Burberry, despite its rich heritage, was struggling with brand dilution and a lack of relevance among younger consumers. Ahrendts recognized that to restore Burberry's prestige, the company needed to embrace digital transformation while preserving its iconic legacy.

- Digital-First Strategy: Ahrendts introduced a digital-first strategy that prioritized the use of technology across all aspects of the business. This included integrating digital technology into marketing, sales, and customer service. Burberry's website was redesigned to be more interactive and visually appealing, reflecting the brand's luxury status while providing an immersive online shopping experience.

- Social Media Engagement: Under Ahrendts' leadership, Burberry became one of the first luxury brands to fully embrace social media. The company used platforms like Facebook, Twitter, Instagram, and YouTube to engage with customers, share behind-the-scenes content, and promote new collections. This proactive approach to social media helped Burberry connect with a younger, tech-savvy audience and build a strong online community.

- Burberry Acoustic: Ahrendts launched Burberry Acoustic, a platform that featured performances by emerging musicians, aligning the brand with the arts and contemporary culture. This initiative not only promoted new talent but also created unique content that resonated with Burberry's audience, enhancing the brand's cultural relevance.

Innovative In-Store Experiences

Ahrendts revolutionized the in-store experience at

Burberry by incorporating cutting-edge technology to create immersive and personalized shopping environments. She understood that physical stores needed to offer something unique that couldn't be replicated online.

- Flagship Store Innovations: Burberry's flagship store on Regent Street in London became a model for luxury retail innovation. The store featured interactive mirrors that turned into screens displaying runway shows and product information, RFID tags on clothing that triggered content on nearby screens, and a seamless integration of online and offline shopping experiences. These innovations provided customers with a dynamic and engaging shopping experience that blended physical and digital elements.

- Burberry World Live: Ahrendts introduced Burberry World Live, an initiative that brought Burberry's digital content to life in its stores. This included live-streaming fashion shows, interactive displays, and virtual reality experiences. The goal was to create a sense of excitement and exclusivity, making the in-store experience more engaging and memorable for customers.

- Personalized Customer Service: Technology was also used to enhance personalized customer service. Sales associates were equipped with iPads to access customer profiles, purchase history, and preferences, enabling them to provide tailored recommendations and a more personalized shopping experience. This focus on personalization helped build stronger relationships with customers and increased brand loyalty.

E-Commerce and Omnichannel Integration

Ahrendts' vision extended beyond physical stores to include a comprehensive e-commerce and omnichannel strategy. She recognized that modern consumers expected a seamless shopping experience across all channels, whether online or offline.

- Enhanced E-Commerce Platform: Burberry's e-commerce platform was revamped to offer a seamless and user-friendly shopping experience. The website featured high-quality images, detailed product descriptions, and customer reviews. It also provided a range of services such as virtual try-ons, live chat support, and flexible delivery options. This focus on enhancing the online shopping experience helped drive significant growth in e-commerce sales.

- Omnichannel Integration: Ahrendts implemented an omnichannel strategy that integrated online and offline channels to provide a cohesive customer experience. This included initiatives like "Click and Collect," where customers could purchase products online and pick them up in-store, and "Endless Aisle," which allowed in-store customers to order products online if they were not available in the store. This seamless integration of channels ensured that customers could interact with Burberry in the way that best suited their needs.

- Data-Driven Insights: Ahrendts leveraged data analytics to gain insights into customer behavior and preferences. This data-driven approach informed marketing strategies, product development, and inventory management, ensuring that Burberry could meet customer demand more effectively. By using data to understand and anticipate customer needs, Burberry was able to provide a more personalized and satisfying shopping experience.

Impact on the Fashion Industry

Ahrendts' innovative use of digital technology at Burberry had a ripple effect across the fashion industry, influencing how other luxury brands approached digital transformation.

- Setting a New Standard: Burberry's success in integrating digital innovation with luxury retail set a new standard for the industry. Other luxury brands began to recognize the importance of embracing technology to stay relevant and competitive. Ahrendts' leadership demonstrated that digital innovation could enhance, rather than detract from, a brand's luxury status.

- Influencing Marketing Strategies: Burberry's

effective use of social media and digital content inspired other brands to adopt similar strategies. The fashion industry saw a shift towards more interactive and engaging marketing campaigns, leveraging digital platforms to reach and connect with a global audience. Ahrendts' approach showed that storytelling and cultural relevance were key components of successful marketing.

- Retail Innovation: The innovations introduced in Burberry's flagship stores influenced how other luxury brands approached the in-store experience. Many brands began to incorporate technology into their retail spaces, creating more immersive and personalized environments. Ahrendts' vision of blending physical and digital experiences became a blueprint for modern luxury retail.

Lessons Learned: Brand Revitalization and Customer Experience

Angela Ahrendts' tenure at Burberry and later at Apple provides valuable lessons in brand revitalization and enhancing the customer experience. Her strategic vision and leadership offer insights for businesses looking to innovate and stay relevant in an increasingly digital world.

Brand Revitalization: Reinventing a Legacy Brand

Ahrendts' success in revitalizing Burberry offers several key lessons for leaders aiming to reinvigorate legacy brands.

- Leveraging Heritage: Ahrendts understood the importance of leveraging Burberry's rich heritage while modernizing its image. She emphasized the brand's iconic symbols, such as the trench coat and check pattern, and integrated them into contemporary designs and marketing campaigns. This approach preserved the brand's authenticity while making it relevant to a new generation of consumers.

- Consistent Brand Messaging: Consistency in brand messaging was a cornerstone of Burberry's revitalization. Ahrendts ensured that the brand's identity was clearly communicated across all touchpoints, from advertising and social media to in-store experiences. Consistent messaging helped build a strong and recognizable brand image, reinforcing customer loyalty and trust.

- Innovation and Tradition: Ahrendts struck a balance between innovation and tradition, recognizing that both were essential for the brand's success. She embraced digital technology and modern marketing techniques while staying true to Burberry's core values and craftsmanship. This balance allowed Burberry to appeal to both traditional and modern consumers.

- Global Expansion: Ahrendts focused on expanding Burberry's presence in key international markets, including Asia and the Middle East. She recognized the importance of tailoring marketing strategies and product offerings to different cultural contexts, ensuring that the brand resonated with diverse audiences. Global expansion was critical for driving growth and establishing Burberry as a leading luxury brand worldwide.

Customer Experience: Enhancing Engagement and Loyalty

Ahrendts' emphasis on enhancing the customer experience provides valuable lessons for businesses looking to build stronger connections with their customers.

- Personalization: Personalization was a key element of Ahrendts' strategy at both Burberry and Apple. She recognized that customers valued personalized experiences and tailored recommendations. By leveraging technology and data, Ahrendts ensured that customers received relevant and personalized service, whether shopping online or in-store. Personalization helped build deeper connections and increased customer loyalty.

- Seamless Integration: Ahrendts' omnichannel approach emphasized the importance of seamless integration between online and offline channels. She understood that customers expected a consistent and cohesive experience across all touchpoints. Initiatives like "Click and Collect" and "Endless Aisle" bridged the gap between digital and physical retail, providing customers with more flexibility and convenience.

- Immersive Experiences: Creating immersive and engaging experiences was central to Ahrendts' strategy. At Burberry, she introduced interactive elements in flagship stores, such as digital mirrors and live-streamed fashion shows. These innovations made the shopping experience more dynamic and memorable. At Apple, the "Today at Apple" program offered educational sessions and workshops, turning stores into community hubs. Immersive experiences fostered a sense of excitement and connection with the brand.

- Customer-Centric Culture: Ahrendts fostered a customer-centric culture within her organizations. She emphasized the importance of understanding and anticipating customer needs, and she empowered employees to deliver exceptional service. This focus on the customer experience permeated every aspect of the business, from product development to marketing and sales. A customer-centric culture ensured that the company consistently delivered value and satisfaction.

Leadership and Vision

Ahrendts' leadership style and vision were instrumental in her success at Burberry and Apple. Her approach offers valuable lessons for leaders aiming to drive innovation and transformation.

- Visionary Leadership: Ahrendts was a visionary leader who could articulate a clear and compelling vision for the future. Her ability to inspire and mobilize teams around a shared vision was a key factor in her success. Leaders should focus on communicating their vision effectively, ensuring that employees understand and are motivated by the company's goals.

- People-Centric Leadership: Ahrendts' people-centric leadership style emphasized the importance of empowering employees and creating a positive work environment. She implemented programs to support employee development, well-being, and engagement. By prioritizing the needs and aspirations of employees, leaders can build strong, motivated teams that are committed to the company's success.

- Inclusive Leadership: Ahrendts was a strong advocate for diversity and inclusion. She promoted initiatives to increase the representation of women and minorities in leadership roles and fostered an inclusive workplace culture. Inclusive leadership leverages diverse perspectives and experiences, driving innovation and enhancing decision-making.

- Ethical Leadership: Ahrendts' commitment to ethical leadership and corporate responsibility was evident in her focus on sustainability and social impact. She believed that businesses had a responsibility to contribute positively to society and the environment. Ethical leadership builds trust and credibility with stakeholders and ensures long-term success.

Creating Shared Value

Ahrendts' approach to leadership and strategy was rooted in the concept of creating shared value, where business success is linked to social and environmental impact.

- Sustainability Initiatives: Ahrendts prioritized sustainability at Burberry, implementing initiatives to reduce the company's environmental footprint and promote ethical practices. Leaders should integrate sustainability into their business strategies, ensuring that their operations contribute to the well-being of the planet and society.

- Community Engagement: Ahrendts emphasized the importance of engaging with local communities and supporting charitable causes. She encouraged Burberry and Apple to invest in education, arts, and social welfare programs. Community engagement strengthens the company's relationship with stakeholders and enhances its social license to operate.

- Ethical Supply Chain: Ahrendts focused on ensuring that Burberry's supply chain adhered to high ethical standards. This included promoting fair labor practices, ensuring safe working conditions, and sourcing materials sustainably. Leaders should prioritize ethical supply chain management to build trust and integrity in their operations.

- Transparency and Accountability: Ahrendts emphasized transparency and accountability in reporting progress towards sustainability and social impact goals. Regular reporting builds trust with stakeholders and demonstrates the company's commitment to continuous improvement. Leaders should prioritize clear and consistent communication to share their organization's achievements and inspire others to take action.

Angela Ahrendts' impact on the luxury retail industry is a testament to her strategic vision, innovative leadership, and commitment to enhancing the customer experience. Her transformative work at Burberry and Apple has set new standards for how brands can integrate digital innovation with traditional retail practices to drive growth and create lasting value.

Ahrendts' success in revitalizing Burberry demonstrates the power of leveraging a brand's heritage while embracing modern technology and innovation. Her focus on consistent brand messaging, personalization, and immersive experiences has influenced how luxury brands approach marketing and customer engagement.

At Apple, Ahrendts redefined the retail experience by creating community-focused, interactive, and seamlessly integrated environments. Her initiatives enhanced customer satisfaction and loyalty, driving significant growth for Apple's retail division.

Angela Ahrendts' story offers valuable lessons for leaders and organizations aiming to navigate the complexities of modern business. By embracing digital innovation, fostering a customer-centric culture, and prioritizing sustainability and ethical practices, businesses can achieve long-term success and make a positive impact on society and the environment. Her legacy as a luxury retail leader continues to inspire and influence the future of retail.

Chapter 10: Sheila Johnson - The Media Magnate

Sheila Crump Johnson was born on January 25, 1949, in McKeesport, Pennsylvania. Growing up in a supportive and ambitious family, she was encouraged to pursue her interests and excel academically. Her father was a neurosurgeon, and her mother was an accountant, setting an example of professional success and dedication. Sheila's upbringing in an intellectually stimulating environment fostered her drive and curiosity, which would later become key factors in her entrepreneurial success.

Early Education and Interests

Johnson's early education was marked by her passion for music and the arts. She was a talented violinist and pursued her love for music with dedication. She attended the University of Illinois, where she majored in music education. Her time in college was not only academically enriching but also a period where she began to understand the broader implications of cultural representation and the power of media.

After graduating from the University of Illinois, Johnson took up a teaching position, becoming the first African American woman to direct a major American symphony. Her role as an educator and conductor provided her with valuable leadership experience and a deep understanding of the importance of representation in the arts.

Transition to Media and Business

In the mid-1970s, Johnson met Robert L. Johnson, and they married in 1969. Together, they ventured into the world of media with a vision to create a platform that would cater to African American audiences. This vision led to the creation of Black Entertainment Television (BET) in 1980. BET was the first cable television network aimed specifically at African American viewers, providing a platform for black culture, music, and entertainment that was largely absent from mainstream media.

Achievements: Co-founding Black Entertainment Television (BET)

Establishing BET

The establishment of BET was a groundbreaking achievement that reshaped the media landscape. Sheila and Robert Johnson faced numerous challenges in the early stages, including securing financing and convincing cable operators to carry their network. However, their determination and clear vision eventually led to BET's successful launch.

- Strategic Vision: Sheila Johnson played a critical role in shaping BET's strategic vision. She recognized the need for a dedicated platform that would celebrate and promote African American culture. This vision guided BET's programming and branding, helping it stand out in a crowded media market.

- Programming and Content: BET's

programming initially focused on music videos, which were a hit with young African American audiences. The network quickly expanded its content to include talk shows, news programs, and original series that addressed issues relevant to the black community. Sheila Johnson's influence was evident in the network's commitment to quality and culturally significant programming.

- Growth and Impact: Under the Johnsons' leadership, BET grew rapidly. By the late 1980s, it had become a major player in the cable television industry. The network's success was a testament to the power of niche programming and the importance of representation in media. BET provided a platform for African American artists, musicians, and producers, significantly impacting the entertainment industry.

- Cultural Influence: BET's influence extended beyond entertainment. The network played a crucial role in shaping cultural narratives and fostering a sense of community among African American viewers. It provided a platform for discussions on social justice, civil rights, and other issues affecting the black community. Sheila Johnson's leadership was instrumental in ensuring that BET remained true to its mission of promoting and celebrating black culture.

Expansion and Diversification

Following the success of BET, Sheila Johnson continued to expand her entrepreneurial ventures, diversifying into sports and hospitality. Her ability to identify opportunities and her strategic approach to business helped her build a diversified and successful portfolio.

Ventures in Sports

- Washington Mystics: In 2005, Sheila Johnson made history by becoming the first African American woman to own a stake in three professional sports teams. She became a co-owner of the Washington Mystics, a Women's National Basketball Association (WNBA) team. Her involvement with the Mystics was driven by her passion for promoting women's sports and providing opportunities for female athletes.

- Washington Wizards and Washington Capitals: Johnson also became a co-owner of the Washington Wizards, an NBA team, and the Washington Capitals, a National Hockey League (NHL) team. Her ownership of these teams marked a significant milestone in the sports industry, highlighting her commitment to diversity and inclusion in professional sports.

- Promotion of Women's Sports: Johnson's involvement in the WNBA and her advocacy for women's sports have had a lasting impact. She has been a vocal supporter of gender equality in sports, emphasizing the importance of providing equal opportunities and resources for female athletes. Her leadership has helped elevate the profile of women's basketball and inspired other women to pursue careers in sports management and ownership.

Ventures in Hospitality

- Salamander Hotels and Resorts: In 2005, Johnson founded Salamander Hotels and Resorts, a luxury hospitality company. The flagship property, Salamander Resort & Spa in Middleburg, Virginia, opened in 2013 and quickly gained recognition for its exceptional service and amenities. Johnson's vision for Salamander was to create unique and luxurious experiences that catered to discerning travelers.

- Expansion of Salamander Portfolio: Under Johnson's leadership, Salamander Hotels and Resorts expanded its portfolio to include properties in various locations, including Florida, South Carolina, and Louisiana. Each property is designed to offer a distinct experience, reflecting the local culture and natural beauty of the area. Johnson's commitment to excellence and attention to detail have been key factors in the success of Salamander's properties.

- Philanthropic Efforts: Johnson's success in the hospitality industry has also enabled her to support various philanthropic efforts. She has been involved in numerous charitable initiatives, focusing on education, healthcare, and social justice. Her philanthropic work reflects her dedication to giving back to the community and making a positive impact on society.

Philanthropy and Advocacy

Sheila Johnson's achievements extend beyond her business ventures. She has been a passionate advocate for social justice, education, and the arts, using her platform and resources to effect positive change.

- Education and Empowerment: Johnson has been a strong supporter of educational initiatives, particularly those aimed at empowering underserved communities. She has donated millions of dollars to various educational institutions and programs, including scholarships for African American students. Her commitment to education reflects her belief in its power to transform lives and create opportunities.

- Social Justice: Johnson has been a vocal advocate for social justice and civil rights. She has used her influence to raise awareness about issues affecting the African American community and to support organizations working towards equality and justice. Her advocacy work includes supporting initiatives aimed at reducing racial disparities in healthcare, education, and criminal justice.

- The Arts: Johnson's passion for the arts has also driven her philanthropic efforts. She has supported numerous cultural and artistic organizations, including the Kennedy Center for the Performing Arts and the Alvin Ailey American Dance Theater. Her contributions have helped promote the arts and provide opportunities for emerging artists.

Lessons Learned: Brand Revitalization and Customer Experience

Sheila Johnson's journey as a media magnate and entrepreneur offers valuable lessons in brand revitalization and enhancing the customer experience. Her strategic vision, innovative thinking, and commitment to excellence provide insights for businesses and leaders looking to achieve success and make a positive impact.

Brand Revitalization: Building and Sustaining a Strong Brand

Johnson's success with BET and her other ventures underscores the importance of building and sustaining a strong brand. Her approach to brand revitalization offers several key lessons.

- Clear Vision and Mission: A clear vision and mission are essential for building a strong brand. Johnson's vision for BET was to create a platform that celebrated and promoted African American culture. This vision guided the network's programming, branding, and strategic decisions. A clear vision helps ensure that all aspects of the brand are aligned and reinforces its identity and purpose.

- Understanding the Audience: Understanding the needs and preferences of the target audience is crucial for brand success. Johnson recognized that there was a lack of representation for African Americans in mainstream media and created BET to fill that gap. By addressing the specific needs of her audience, she built a loyal and engaged viewer base. Businesses should conduct thorough market research to understand their audience and tailor their offerings accordingly.

- Consistency and Quality: Consistency and quality are key factors in building and sustaining a strong brand. Johnson ensured that BET's programming and content consistently reflected the network's mission and values. High-quality production and compelling content helped establish BET's reputation as a trusted and influential media platform. Consistency and quality build trust and credibility with customers, reinforcing the brand's position in the market.

- Innovation and Adaptability: Innovation and adaptability are essential for brand revitalization. Johnson embraced new technologies and platforms to reach and engage with her audience. She recognized the importance of staying relevant in a rapidly changing media landscape. Businesses should be open to innovation and willing to adapt to changing market conditions to remain competitive and sustain their brand's success.

Customer Experience: Enhancing Engagement and Loyalty

Johnson's focus on enhancing the customer experience has been a key factor in her success. Her approach to customer experience provides valuable lessons for businesses looking to build stronger connections with their customers.

- Personalization: Personalization is a critical component of a positive customer experience. Johnson understood the importance of providing content and experiences that resonated with her audience. BET's programming was tailored to address the interests and concerns of African American viewers. Personalization helps build deeper connections with customers and increases their loyalty to the brand.

- Engagement and Interaction: Engaging with customers and encouraging interaction is essential for building a strong customer relationship. Johnson's initiatives, such as Burberry Acoustic and "Today at Apple," created opportunities for customers to engage with the brand and each other. These initiatives fostered a sense of community and enhanced customer loyalty. Businesses should create opportunities for customers to interact with the brand and provide feedback.

- Seamless Integration: Seamless integration of online and offline experiences enhances the customer journey. Johnson's omnichannel strategies at Burberry and Apple ensured that customers received a consistent and cohesive experience across all touchpoints. This integration provided convenience and flexibility, improving overall customer satisfaction. Businesses should aim to create a seamless experience for customers, regardless of how they choose to interact with the brand.

- Commitment to Excellence: A commitment to excellence is essential for delivering a superior customer experience. Johnson's focus on quality and attention to detail were evident in all her ventures, from BET to Salamander Hotels and Resorts. Providing exceptional service and products builds trust and satisfaction, encouraging repeat business and positive word-of-mouth. Businesses should strive for excellence in all aspects of their operations to enhance the customer experience.

Sheila Johnson's remarkable journey from a music educator to a media magnate and successful entrepreneur is a testament to her strategic vision, innovative thinking, and unwavering commitment to excellence. Her achievements in co-founding BET, pioneering ventures in sports and hospitality, and her philanthropic efforts have left a lasting impact on the media industry and beyond.

Johnson's success with BET transformed the media

landscape, providing a platform for African American culture and addressing the lack of representation in mainstream media. Her strategic approach to brand revitalization and customer experience set new standards for the industry, demonstrating the power of a clear vision, understanding the audience, and embracing innovation.

Her ventures in sports and hospitality further showcased her ability to identify opportunities and build successful enterprises across different industries. Johnson's commitment to promoting diversity, supporting women's sports, and delivering exceptional customer experiences has been instrumental in her success.

Beyond her business achievements, Johnson's philanthropy and advocacy work reflect her dedication to making a positive impact on society. Her support for education, social justice, and the arts has contributed to the betterment of communities and inspired others to follow her example.

Sheila Johnson's story offers valuable lessons for leaders and entrepreneurs aiming to achieve success and make a difference. By prioritizing brand revitalization, enhancing the customer experience, and maintaining a commitment to excellence, businesses can create lasting value and positively impact their industry and society. Johnson's legacy as a media magnate and visionary leader continues to inspire and influence the next generation of innovators and changemakers.

Impact on Industry: Paving the Way for African

American Media and Entrepreneurship
Transforming the Media Landscape

Sheila Johnson's co-founding of Black Entertainment Television (BET) alongside her then-husband Robert L. Johnson marked a significant milestone in the history of American media. BET, launched in 1980, was the first cable television network dedicated exclusively to African American audiences. Its creation was a response to the lack of representation and programming that catered specifically to black viewers, who were often marginalized in mainstream media.

Filling a Critical Gap

At a time when African American representation on television was minimal and often stereotypical, BET provided a platform for black voices, stories, and culture. This had several profound impacts on the media landscape and the African American community:

- Representation and Visibility: BET gave African Americans a significant and dedicated presence on television. It allowed black artists, actors, musicians, and public figures to showcase their talents and tell their stories in a way that resonated with their community. This representation was crucial in fostering a sense of pride and identity among black viewers.

- Cultural Celebration: BET celebrated African American culture through a variety of programming, including music videos, talk shows, news segments, and original series. It highlighted the richness and diversity of black culture, from hip-hop and R&B music to black history and achievements. This cultural celebration helped combat negative stereotypes and provided a more accurate portrayal of the black experience.

- Economic Opportunities: The success of BET created economic opportunities within the African American community. It provided jobs and career opportunities for black professionals in the media industry, from on-screen talent to behind-the-scenes roles in production, marketing, and management. This economic empowerment had a ripple effect, contributing to the growth of black entrepreneurship and economic independence.

Innovative Programming and Content

Under Sheila Johnson's leadership, BET developed a range of innovative programming that addressed the interests and needs of its audience. The network's content strategy was designed to be both entertaining and informative, reflecting the diverse tastes and concerns of black viewers.

- Music Programming: Music was a cornerstone of BET's programming. Shows like "Video Soul" and "Rap City" became iconic platforms for showcasing African American music and artists. These programs helped launch the careers of many musicians and provided a space for black music to thrive. BET's focus on music also helped shape the broader music industry by influencing trends and highlighting emerging talent.

- News and Information: BET recognized the importance of providing news and information relevant to the African American community. Programs like "BET News" and "BET Nightly News" covered stories and issues that were often overlooked by mainstream media. These shows addressed topics such as civil rights, social justice, and political developments, helping to inform and empower black viewers.

- Original Programming: In addition to music and news, BET developed original programming that resonated with its audience. Shows like "Teen Summit" provided a platform for young people to discuss issues affecting their lives, while sitcoms and drama series offered relatable stories and characters. This original content helped differentiate BET from other networks and built a loyal viewer base.

Influence on the Broader Media Industry

BET's success had a significant impact on the broader media industry. It demonstrated the viability and profitability of targeting niche audiences and paved the way for other minority-focused media outlets. BET's influence extended beyond African American media, inspiring networks and content creators to recognize and cater to diverse audiences.

- Setting Precedents: BET set a precedent for

minority-focused media networks. Its success showed that there was a substantial market for content that catered to specific cultural and demographic groups. This realization encouraged the development of other minority-owned media ventures and niche programming.

- Changing Perceptions: BET played a crucial role in changing perceptions of African American media and culture. By showcasing positive and diverse representations of black life, the network helped challenge stereotypes and promote a more nuanced understanding of the African American experience. This shift in perception had a broader societal impact, contributing to greater acceptance and appreciation of black culture.

- Economic Impact: BET's success also demonstrated the economic potential of minority-focused media. The network's profitability attracted the attention of investors and advertisers, leading to increased investment in minority-owned media enterprises. This economic impact extended beyond the media industry, fostering growth and development in other sectors of the black economy.

Empowering African American Entrepreneurs

Sheila Johnson's impact on the industry extended beyond media to entrepreneurship. Her success with BET and subsequent ventures in sports, hospitality, and other fields provided a powerful example for aspiring African American entrepreneurs. Johnson's career illustrates the importance of diversification and seizing opportunities, offering valuable lessons for business leaders.

Lessons Learned: Diversification and Seizing Opportunities

Embracing Diversification

Sheila Johnson's career is a testament to the power of diversification. After the success of BET, she did not rest on her laurels but instead expanded her business interests into new and varied fields. This strategic diversification not only increased her wealth but also mitigated risk and created new opportunities for impact and influence.

Ventures in Sports

Johnson's entry into the sports industry marked a significant expansion of her entrepreneurial portfolio. Her involvement in professional sports demonstrated her ability to identify and capitalize on new opportunities.

- **Washington Mystics:** In 2005, Johnson became the first African American woman to own a stake in three professional sports teams. She co-owned the Washington Mystics, a Women's National Basketball Association (WNBA) team. Her investment in the Mystics was driven by her passion for promoting women's sports and providing opportunities for female athletes.

This venture highlighted her commitment to gender equality and diversity in sports.

- Washington Wizards and Washington Capitals: Johnson also became a co-owner of the Washington Wizards (NBA) and the Washington Capitals (NHL). Her ownership of these teams marked a significant milestone in the sports industry, showcasing her ability to navigate and succeed in traditionally male-dominated fields. Johnson's involvement in professional sports not only diversified her business interests but also provided a platform for advocating for diversity and inclusion in athletics.

Ventures in Hospitality

Johnson's foray into the hospitality industry further demonstrated her entrepreneurial versatility. In 2005, she founded Salamander Hotels and Resorts, a luxury hospitality company that quickly gained recognition for its exceptional service and amenities.

- Salamander Resort & Spa: The flagship property, Salamander Resort & Spa in Middleburg, Virginia, opened in 2013. The resort's success was a testament to Johnson's vision and attention to detail. Salamander Resort & Spa became known for its luxurious accommodations, world-class amenities, and unique experiences. Johnson's commitment to excellence set a high standard for the hospitality industry.

- Expansion and Impact: Under Johnson's leadership, Salamander Hotels and Resorts expanded its portfolio to include properties in various locations, including Florida, South Carolina, and Louisiana. Each property was designed to offer a distinct experience, reflecting the local culture and natural beauty of the area. Johnson's focus on creating unique and luxurious experiences helped differentiate Salamander from other hospitality brands.

- Philanthropy and Community Engagement: Johnson's success in hospitality also enabled her to support various philanthropic efforts. She has been involved in numerous charitable initiatives, focusing on education, healthcare, and social justice. Her philanthropic work reflects her dedication to giving back to the community and making a positive impact on society.

Ventures in Media and Entertainment

Johnson's career in media did not end with BET. She continued to explore new opportunities in the industry, leveraging her experience and expertise to create impactful ventures.

- TV One: After BET, Johnson co-founded TV One, a cable network targeting African American adults. TV One offered a mix of original programming, classic sitcoms, and movies that resonated with its audience. The network's success demonstrated Johnson's ability to identify and fill gaps in the media market.

- Film Production: Johnson also ventured into film production, supporting projects that highlighted African American stories and talent. Her involvement in the film industry helped bring diverse perspectives to the screen and provided opportunities for black filmmakers and actors.

Lessons from Diversification

Johnson's diversification strategy offers valuable lessons for entrepreneurs and business leaders.

- Identifying Opportunities: Johnson's ability to identify and capitalize on new opportunities was key to her success. She recognized emerging trends and gaps in the market, positioning herself to take advantage of them. Entrepreneurs should stay informed about industry developments and be ready to seize opportunities as they arise.

- Risk Management: Diversification helps mitigate risk by spreading investments across different industries and sectors. Johnson's ventures in sports, hospitality, and media ensured that her financial success was not tied to a single industry. This approach reduces vulnerability to market fluctuations and increases overall stability.

- Leveraging Expertise: Johnson leveraged her expertise and experience from BET to succeed in other ventures. Her knowledge of media, branding, and customer engagement was transferable to other industries, providing a strong foundation for her entrepreneurial endeavors. Entrepreneurs should build on their existing skills and experience while exploring new opportunities.

- Commitment to Excellence: Johnson's commitment to excellence was evident in all her ventures. Whether in media, sports, or hospitality, she prioritized quality and attention to detail. This focus on excellence helped build strong brands and create lasting value. Entrepreneurs should strive for excellence in all aspects of their business to achieve long-term success.

Seizing Opportunities

Sheila Johnson's career is also a powerful example of the importance of seizing opportunities. Her ability to recognize and act on potential opportunities has been a driving force behind her success.

Strategic Vision and Leadership

Johnson's strategic vision and leadership have been instrumental in her ability to seize opportunities and drive growth.

- Visionary Leadership: Johnson's visionary leadership was key to the success of BET and her other ventures. She had a clear vision for what she wanted to achieve and was able to articulate it to her team and stakeholders. This clarity of vision provided direction and motivation, helping her seize opportunities and navigate challenges.

- Bold Decision-Making: Johnson was not afraid to make bold decisions and take calculated risks. Her decision to co-found BET and later expand into sports and hospitality were ambitious moves that required confidence and conviction. Entrepreneurs should be willing to take risks and make bold decisions to capitalize on opportunities.

- Adaptability and Resilience: Johnson's adaptability and resilience enabled her to navigate changing market conditions and overcome obstacles. She was able to pivot and adjust her strategies as needed, ensuring that her ventures remained competitive and successful. Entrepreneurs should cultivate adaptability and resilience to thrive in dynamic environments.

Building Strong Networks

Johnson's success was also supported by her ability to build strong networks and partnerships.

- Collaborative Partnerships: Johnson recognized the value of collaborative partnerships in achieving her goals. She worked with industry experts, investors, and stakeholders to build and grow her ventures. These partnerships provided valuable resources, expertise, and support. Entrepreneurs should seek out and cultivate strategic partnerships to enhance their capabilities and reach.

- Mentorship and Support: Johnson's career was influenced by mentors and supporters who provided guidance and encouragement. She, in turn, became a mentor and advocate for others, helping to pave the way for future generations of entrepreneurs. Entrepreneurs should seek mentorship and be willing to mentor others, creating a supportive ecosystem for success.

- Community Engagement: Johnson's commitment to community engagement was a key factor in her success. She built strong relationships with the communities she served, ensuring that her ventures were aligned with their needs and values. This engagement fostered loyalty and trust, enhancing the reputation and impact of her ventures. Entrepreneurs should prioritize community engagement and build meaningful connections with their audience.

Creating Lasting Impact

Johnson's ability to seize opportunities has not only driven her financial success but also created lasting impact and change.

- Empowering Others: Johnson's ventures have created opportunities and empowerment for others. BET provided a platform for African

American voices and talent, while her involvement in sports and hospitality has promoted diversity and inclusion. Johnson's legacy includes the empowerment of individuals and communities, inspiring others to pursue their dreams and achieve success.

- Driving Social Change: Johnson's work has contributed to driving social change and advancing equality. Her advocacy for education, social justice, and the arts has made a positive impact on society, addressing systemic issues and promoting progress. Entrepreneurs should recognize the potential for their ventures to drive social change and contribute to a better world.

- Building a Legacy: Johnson's career is a testament to the power of vision, determination, and action. She has built a legacy of success and impact that will continue to inspire and influence future generations. Entrepreneurs should strive to create a lasting legacy by pursuing their vision with passion and purpose.

Sheila Johnson's remarkable journey from co-founding BET to her ventures in sports, hospitality, and beyond is a testament to her strategic vision, innovative thinking, and commitment to excellence. Her impact on the media industry, African American entrepreneurship, and broader society is profound and far-reaching.

Johnson's success with BET transformed the media

landscape, providing a platform for African American culture and creating economic opportunities within the black community. Her strategic approach to diversification and ability to seize opportunities have driven her success in various industries, demonstrating the importance of adaptability, risk management, and strategic vision.

Johnson's legacy includes her contributions to social justice, education, and the arts, reflecting her dedication to making a positive impact on society. Her career offers valuable lessons for entrepreneurs and business leaders, emphasizing the importance of diversification, seizing opportunities, and creating lasting value.

Sheila Johnson's story is an inspiration for aspiring entrepreneurs and leaders, showcasing the power of determination, innovation, and excellence in achieving success and driving change. Her legacy as a media magnate and visionary entrepreneur continues to influence and inspire future generations, paving the way for a more inclusive and equitable world.

Chapter 11: Safra Catz - The Tech Leader

Safra Catz's journey in the technology sector is a remarkable story of perseverance, strategic acumen, and leadership. Born on December 1, 1961, in Holon, Israel, Catz immigrated to the United States at a young age. Her family settled in Brookline, Massachusetts, where she spent her formative years. Growing up in an immigrant family, Catz learned the values of hard work, resilience, and determination early on.

Early Life and Education

Catz's academic journey was marked by excellence and ambition. She attended Brookline High School, where she excelled in her studies. Her passion for learning and her determination to succeed led her to the University of Pennsylvania, where she earned a bachelor's degree in Economics from the Wharton School of Business in 1983. Catz's time at Wharton provided her with a strong foundation in finance and business, skills that would prove invaluable in her future career.

After completing her undergraduate studies, Catz pursued a Juris Doctor degree from the University of Pennsylvania Law School, graduating in 1986. Her legal education equipped her with a deep understanding of corporate law and regulatory issues, further enhancing her capabilities as a future business leader.

Early Career and Transition to Technology

Following law school, Catz began her career in the legal field. She joined the prestigious law firm of Donaldson, Lufkin & Jenrette (DLJ) as an investment banker. Her role at DLJ involved working on mergers and acquisitions, public offerings, and other financial transactions. This experience provided Catz with valuable insights into the world of corporate finance and strategic business operations.

Catz's transition from law to technology came in the late 1990s when she joined Oracle Corporation. Her decision to move to Oracle was driven by her desire to work in a dynamic and fast-growing industry. Oracle, a global leader in database software and technology, offered Catz the opportunity to leverage her financial expertise and strategic insights in a new and challenging environment.

Joining Oracle Corporation

In 1999, Safra Catz joined Oracle Corporation as Senior Vice President. Her initial responsibilities included overseeing Oracle's corporate finance and legal departments. Catz's deep understanding of finance and her ability to navigate complex legal and regulatory issues quickly earned her the respect of her colleagues and superiors.

Strategic Acquisitions and Growth

One of Catz's most significant contributions to Oracle has been her role in spearheading the company's aggressive acquisition strategy. Under her leadership, Oracle has completed more than 130 acquisitions, transforming the company into a diversified technology powerhouse.

- PeopleSoft Acquisition: One of the most notable acquisitions under Catz's leadership was the hostile takeover of PeopleSoft in 2005. This $10.3 billion deal was highly contentious, involving legal battles and regulatory scrutiny. Catz's strategic acumen and negotiation skills were instrumental in navigating the complexities of the acquisition and ultimately securing PeopleSoft, which significantly expanded Oracle's enterprise software offerings.

- BEA Systems Acquisition: In 2008, Catz played a key role in Oracle's acquisition of BEA Systems for $8.5 billion. This acquisition strengthened Oracle's position in the middleware market, enhancing its ability to provide integrated software solutions to its customers.

- Sun Microsystems Acquisition: Another major acquisition was Sun Microsystems in 2010 for $7.4 billion. This deal brought Java, one of the most widely used programming languages, under Oracle's umbrella and expanded the company's hardware and software capabilities. The acquisition of Sun Microsystems positioned Oracle as a more comprehensive technology provider, offering a full stack of hardware and software solutions.

Leadership Style and Influence

Safra Catz's leadership style is characterized by her strategic vision, analytical rigor, and no-nonsense approach. She is known for her ability to make tough decisions and her unwavering focus on achieving Oracle's strategic objectives.

- Strategic Vision: Catz's strategic vision has been a driving force behind Oracle's growth and transformation. She has consistently emphasized the importance of innovation, operational efficiency, and market expansion. Her ability to anticipate industry trends and adapt Oracle's strategy accordingly has been critical to the company's success.

- Analytical Rigor: Catz's background in finance and law has instilled in her a strong analytical mindset. She is known for her attention to detail and her ability to thoroughly analyze complex business scenarios. This analytical rigor enables her to make informed decisions that align with Oracle's long-term goals.

- No-Nonsense Approach: Catz's no-nonsense approach to leadership has earned her a reputation for being direct and results-oriented. She is known for her straightforward communication style and her focus on accountability. This approach has helped foster a culture of transparency and high performance at Oracle.

Achievements: Rising to Become CEO of Oracle Corporation

Safra Catz's rise to the position of CEO of Oracle Corporation is a testament to her exceptional leadership and strategic capabilities. Her journey to the top of one of the world's largest technology companies is marked by significant achievements and transformative contributions.

Becoming CEO

In September 2014, Safra Catz was appointed co-CEO of Oracle alongside Mark Hurd. This appointment marked a significant milestone in her career and reflected her deep understanding of Oracle's business and her proven leadership abilities. Following Mark Hurd's passing in 2019, Catz became the sole CEO of Oracle, further solidifying her leadership role.

- Financial Stewardship: As CFO and later as co-CEO and CEO, Catz has been responsible for Oracle's financial strategy and performance. Under her leadership, Oracle has consistently delivered strong financial results, demonstrating her ability to manage the company's finances effectively and drive profitability.

- Cloud Transformation: One of the most significant achievements under Catz's leadership has been Oracle's transformation into a cloud computing powerhouse. Recognizing the shift towards cloud-based solutions, Catz has overseen significant investments in Oracle's cloud infrastructure and services. This strategic focus on the cloud has positioned Oracle as a key player in the rapidly growing cloud computing market.

Driving Cloud Innovation

Catz's leadership has been instrumental in driving Oracle's cloud innovation and expanding its cloud offerings. Her strategic initiatives have enabled Oracle to compete with industry giants like Amazon Web Services (AWS) and Microsoft Azure.

- Oracle Cloud Infrastructure (OCI): Under Catz's leadership, Oracle has made significant advancements in its cloud infrastructure. OCI provides a comprehensive suite of cloud services, including computing, storage, and networking, designed to meet the needs of enterprise customers. Oracle's focus on delivering high-performance, secure, and scalable cloud solutions has attracted a growing number of customers.

- Software as a Service (SaaS): Catz has also driven the expansion of Oracle's SaaS offerings. Oracle's suite of SaaS applications, including ERP, HCM, and CRM, provides businesses with powerful tools to manage their operations, human resources, and customer relationships. These applications are designed to integrate seamlessly with Oracle's cloud infrastructure, offering a unified and efficient solution for customers.

- Autonomous Database: One of Oracle's groundbreaking innovations under Catz's leadership is the Autonomous Database. This self-driving database leverages artificial intelligence and machine learning to automate many of the administrative tasks associated with database management. The Autonomous Database enhances performance, security, and reliability while reducing the need for manual intervention.

Expanding Global Reach

Catz's strategic vision has also focused on expanding Oracle's global reach. She has overseen the company's expansion into new markets and regions, enhancing its global presence and customer base.

- Emerging Markets: Catz has recognized the growth potential in emerging markets and has driven Oracle's efforts to expand its footprint in these regions. Oracle has established data centers and offices in key emerging markets, providing local businesses with access to its cloud services and technology solutions.

- Strategic Partnerships: Under Catz's leadership, Oracle has forged strategic partnerships with other technology companies, governments, and industry leaders. These partnerships have facilitated Oracle's entry into new markets and enhanced its ability to deliver innovative solutions to customers worldwide.

Commitment to Corporate Responsibility

Safra Catz's leadership is also characterized by her commitment to corporate responsibility and ethical business practices. She has emphasized the importance of sustainability, diversity, and social impact in Oracle's operations.

- Sustainability Initiatives: Oracle has implemented various sustainability initiatives under Catz's leadership. The company has focused on reducing its environmental footprint, promoting energy efficiency, and adopting sustainable business practices. Oracle's data centers, for example, are designed to be energy-efficient and environmentally friendly.

- Diversity and Inclusion: Catz has been a strong advocate for diversity and inclusion within Oracle. She has supported initiatives aimed at increasing the representation of women and minorities in the technology industry. Oracle's diversity and inclusion programs focus on creating an inclusive workplace culture and providing opportunities for underrepresented groups.

- Social Impact: Oracle has also engaged in numerous social impact initiatives under Catz's leadership. The company supports educational programs, disaster relief efforts, and community development projects. Oracle's social impact initiatives aim to leverage technology for positive change and contribute to the well-being of communities around the world.

Navigating Challenges and Leading Through Change

Catz's tenure as CEO of Oracle has not been without challenges. The rapidly evolving technology landscape, increasing competition, and economic uncertainties have required Catz to navigate complex and dynamic environments.

- Adapting to Industry Changes: The technology industry is characterized by rapid innovation and change. Catz has demonstrated her ability to adapt to these changes and position Oracle for continued success. Her focus on cloud computing, data analytics, and artificial intelligence has ensured that Oracle remains at the forefront of technological advancements.

- Competitive Landscape: Oracle faces intense competition from other technology giants. Catz's strategic initiatives have enabled Oracle to differentiate itself and compete effectively. Her emphasis on innovation, customer-centric solutions, and strategic partnerships has strengthened Oracle's competitive position.

- Economic Uncertainties: The global economy has faced numerous uncertainties, including economic downturns and geopolitical challenges. Catz's financial acumen and strategic planning have helped Oracle navigate these uncertainties and maintain its financial stability and growth.

Lessons in Leadership

Safra Catz's leadership journey offers valuable lessons for aspiring leaders and business professionals.

- Strategic Vision: Catz's ability to articulate and execute a clear strategic vision has been instrumental in her success. Leaders should focus on developing a long-term vision that aligns with their organization's goals and values.

- Analytical Rigor: Catz's analytical mindset and attention to detail have enabled her to make informed decisions. Leaders should cultivate strong analytical skills and use data-driven insights to guide their decision-making.

- Adaptability: The ability to adapt to changing circumstances and industry trends is critical for success. Catz's adaptability has allowed her to navigate complex challenges and drive innovation. Leaders should embrace change and be willing to pivot their strategies when necessary.

- Commitment to Excellence: Catz's commitment to excellence is evident in all aspects of her leadership. Leaders should strive for excellence in their operations, products, and customer service to build a strong and reputable brand.

- Ethical Leadership: Catz's emphasis on

corporate responsibility and ethical business practices sets a positive example for leaders. Leaders should prioritize ethical conduct, sustainability, and social impact in their decision-making.

Safra Catz's journey in the technology sector and her rise to become CEO of Oracle Corporation is a story of exceptional leadership, strategic vision, and transformative impact. Her contributions to Oracle's growth, innovation, and global reach have solidified her position as a leading figure in the technology industry.

Catz's achievements in driving Oracle's cloud transformation, expanding its global presence, and fostering a culture of corporate responsibility have left a lasting legacy. Her leadership style, characterized by analytical rigor, adaptability, and a no-nonsense approach, offers valuable lessons for business leaders and professionals.

As Oracle continues to evolve and adapt to the changing technology landscape, Catz's strategic vision and leadership will remain a guiding force. Her commitment to excellence, innovation, and ethical business practices will continue to shape Oracle's success and influence the broader technology industry.

Safra Catz's story is an inspiration for aspiring leaders and entrepreneurs, showcasing the power of determination, strategic thinking, and leadership in achieving success and driving positive change. Her legacy as a tech leader and visionary continues to inspire and influence future generations of business leaders.

Impact on Industry: Influencing Corporate Strategy and Tech Innovation

Safra Catz's tenure at Oracle Corporation has been marked by her profound impact on corporate strategy and technology innovation. Since joining Oracle in 1999 and rising to the role of CEO, Catz has played a pivotal role in shaping the company's strategic direction, driving significant transformations, and positioning Oracle as a leader in the technology sector.

Revamping Corporate Strategy

Catz's influence on Oracle's corporate strategy has been multifaceted, encompassing aggressive acquisition strategies, a strong focus on cloud computing, and an unwavering commitment to innovation and customer-centric solutions.

- Aggressive Acquisition Strategy: One of Catz's most notable contributions to Oracle's corporate strategy has been her aggressive approach to acquisitions. Under her leadership, Oracle has acquired over 130 companies, strategically expanding its product portfolio and market reach. These acquisitions have been instrumental in strengthening Oracle's position in various technology sectors and enhancing its capabilities.

- PeopleSoft Acquisition: The 2005 acquisition

of PeopleSoft for $10.3 billion was a landmark deal that significantly expanded Oracle's enterprise software offerings. The acquisition was highly contentious, involving legal battles and regulatory scrutiny. Catz's negotiation skills and strategic acumen were crucial in navigating these challenges and successfully integrating PeopleSoft into Oracle's operations.

- BEA Systems Acquisition: In 2008, Oracle acquired BEA Systems for $8.5 billion, bolstering its middleware solutions and enhancing its ability to provide integrated software solutions to enterprise customers. This acquisition further solidified Oracle's position in the middleware market.

- Sun Microsystems Acquisition: The acquisition of Sun Microsystems in 2010 for $7.4 billion was another significant milestone. This deal brought Java, one of the most widely used programming languages, under Oracle's umbrella and expanded the company's hardware and software capabilities. The acquisition positioned Oracle as a more comprehensive technology provider, offering a full stack of hardware and software solutions.

- Focus on Cloud Computing: Recognizing the industry's shift towards cloud-based solutions, Catz has been a driving force behind Oracle's transformation into a cloud computing powerhouse. She has overseen substantial investments in Oracle's cloud infrastructure and services, positioning the company as a key player in the cloud computing market.

- Oracle Cloud Infrastructure (OCI): Under Catz's leadership, Oracle has made significant advancements in its cloud infrastructure. OCI provides a comprehensive suite of cloud services, including computing, storage, and networking, designed to meet the needs of enterprise customers. Oracle's focus on delivering high-performance, secure, and scalable cloud solutions has attracted a growing number of customers.

- Software as a Service (SaaS): Catz has also driven the expansion of Oracle's SaaS offerings. Oracle's suite of SaaS applications, including ERP, HCM, and CRM, provides businesses with powerful tools to manage their operations, human resources, and customer relationships. These applications are designed to integrate seamlessly with Oracle's cloud infrastructure, offering a unified and efficient solution for customers.

- Innovation and Customer-Centric Solutions: Catz's strategic vision has consistently emphasized innovation and customer-centric solutions. She has championed the development of cutting-edge technologies and products that address the evolving needs of Oracle's customers.

- Autonomous Database: One of Oracle's groundbreaking innovations under Catz's leadership is the Autonomous Database. This self-driving database leverages artificial intelligence and machine learning to automate many of the administrative tasks associated with database management. The Autonomous Database enhances performance, security, and reliability while reducing the need for manual intervention, setting a new standard in the industry.

- Data Analytics and AI: Oracle has also invested heavily in data analytics and artificial intelligence, developing advanced solutions that enable businesses to gain insights from their data and make informed decisions. These innovations have positioned Oracle as a leader in the rapidly growing fields of data analytics and AI.

Enhancing Oracle's Global Reach

Catz's strategic initiatives have not only transformed Oracle's product portfolio but also expanded its global reach. She has overseen the company's expansion into new markets and regions, enhancing its presence and customer base worldwide.

- Emerging Markets: Catz has recognized the growth potential in emerging markets and has driven Oracle's efforts to expand its footprint in these regions. Oracle has established data centers and offices in key emerging markets, providing local businesses with access to its cloud services and technology solutions. This expansion has enabled Oracle to tap into new revenue streams and diversify its customer base.

- Strategic Partnerships: Under Catz's leadership, Oracle has forged strategic partnerships with other technology companies, governments, and industry leaders. These partnerships have facilitated Oracle's entry into new markets and enhanced its ability to deliver innovative solutions to customers worldwide. Collaborations with companies like Microsoft, Google, and Salesforce have strengthened Oracle's ecosystem and extended its reach.

Commitment to Corporate Responsibility

Catz's influence on Oracle's corporate strategy extends beyond financial performance and market expansion. She has emphasized the importance of corporate responsibility, sustainability, and ethical business practices.

- Sustainability Initiatives: Oracle has implemented various sustainability initiatives under Catz's leadership. The company has focused on reducing its environmental footprint, promoting energy efficiency, and adopting sustainable business practices. Oracle's data centers, for example, are designed to be energy-efficient and environmentally friendly. Catz's commitment to sustainability reflects her understanding of the long-term impact of corporate actions on the environment.

- Diversity and Inclusion: Catz has been a strong

advocate for diversity and inclusion within Oracle. She has supported initiatives aimed at increasing the representation of women and minorities in the technology industry. Oracle's diversity and inclusion programs focus on creating an inclusive workplace culture and providing opportunities for underrepresented groups. Catz's leadership in this area has helped foster a more diverse and dynamic workforce.

- Social Impact: Oracle has also engaged in numerous social impact initiatives under Catz's leadership. The company supports educational programs, disaster relief efforts, and community development projects. Oracle's social impact initiatives aim to leverage technology for positive change and contribute to the well-being of communities around the world. Catz's commitment to social responsibility underscores her belief in the role of business as a force for good.

Lessons Learned: Strategic Leadership and Financial Acumen

Safra Catz's leadership journey offers valuable lessons in strategic leadership, particularly in the context of navigating the complex and dynamic technology industry. Her ability to develop and execute a clear strategic vision has been instrumental in Oracle's success.

Visionary Leadership

- Articulating a Clear Vision: Catz's ability to articulate a clear and compelling vision for Oracle's future has been a cornerstone of her leadership. She has consistently communicated the company's strategic goals and priorities, ensuring that employees, stakeholders, and customers understand and are aligned with the company's direction. This clarity of vision has provided a sense of purpose and direction, motivating the organization to achieve its objectives.

- Long-Term Thinking: Catz's strategic leadership is characterized by her focus on long-term thinking. She has emphasized the importance of investing in innovation, infrastructure, and talent to drive sustainable growth. By taking a long-term perspective, Catz has ensured that Oracle remains resilient and competitive in a rapidly changing industry.

Adaptability and Resilience

- Navigating Industry Changes: The technology industry is characterized by rapid innovation and change. Catz's ability to adapt to these changes and position Oracle for continued success has been a key factor in her leadership. She has demonstrated a willingness to pivot strategies, embrace new technologies, and explore emerging markets. This adaptability has enabled Oracle to stay ahead of industry trends and seize new opportunities.

- Resilience in the Face of Challenges: Catz's resilience in the face of challenges has been evident throughout her tenure at Oracle. She has navigated complex mergers and acquisitions, regulatory scrutiny, and economic uncertainties with confidence and determination. Her resilience has inspired confidence within the organization and has helped Oracle overcome obstacles and achieve its strategic goals.

Innovation and Customer-Centric Solutions

- Fostering a Culture of Innovation: Catz has championed a culture of innovation at Oracle, encouraging employees to think creatively and develop cutting-edge solutions. She has supported investments in research and development, ensuring that Oracle remains at the forefront of technological advancements. This focus on innovation has enabled Oracle to deliver products and services that meet the evolving needs of its customers.

- Customer-Centric Approach: Catz's strategic leadership has been characterized by a customer-centric approach. She has emphasized the importance of understanding and addressing customer needs, developing solutions that provide real value. By prioritizing customer satisfaction and building strong relationships, Catz has strengthened Oracle's brand and competitive position.

Financial Acumen

Safra Catz's financial acumen has been a driving force behind Oracle's financial success and stability. Her expertise in corporate finance, strategic planning, and financial management has been instrumental in achieving the company's financial goals.

Financial Stewardship

- Effective Financial Management: Catz's role as CFO and later as CEO has involved overseeing Oracle's financial strategy and performance. She has demonstrated effective financial management, ensuring that the company maintains a strong balance sheet, generates consistent revenue growth, and delivers value to shareholders. Her financial stewardship has been characterized by disciplined cost management, strategic investments, and prudent risk management.

- Driving Profitability: Under Catz's leadership, Oracle has consistently delivered strong financial results. She has implemented strategies to drive profitability, including optimizing operational efficiency, streamlining processes, and leveraging economies of scale. Catz's focus on profitability has enabled Oracle to reinvest in innovation and growth initiatives.

Strategic Acquisitions

- Value-Driven Acquisitions: Catz's approach to acquisitions has been driven by a focus on value creation. She has identified and pursued acquisitions that align with Oracle's strategic goals, enhance its product portfolio, and expand its market reach. By integrating acquired companies effectively, Catz has maximized the value of these acquisitions and strengthened Oracle's competitive position.

- Synergy Realization: Catz's financial acumen has been critical in realizing synergies from acquisitions. She has implemented strategies to integrate acquired companies, optimize resources, and achieve cost savings. This focus on synergy realization has enhanced the financial performance of acquired businesses and contributed to Oracle's overall growth.

Capital Allocation

- Strategic Investments: Catz's expertise in capital allocation has enabled Oracle to make strategic investments in technology, infrastructure, and talent. She has prioritized investments that drive innovation, enhance operational efficiency, and support long-term growth. This strategic approach to capital allocation has ensured that Oracle remains competitive and positioned for future success.

- Shareholder Value: Catz's financial acumen has also been evident in her commitment to delivering value to shareholders. Oracle has implemented share buyback programs and dividend policies that reflect the company's financial strength and commitment to returning capital to shareholders. These initiatives have enhanced shareholder value and demonstrated Catz's focus on financial performance.

Lessons in Financial Acumen

Safra Catz's financial acumen offers valuable lessons for business leaders and financial professionals.

- Strategic Planning: Effective financial management requires strategic planning and a clear understanding of the company's financial goals. Leaders should develop comprehensive financial strategies that align with the company's overall vision and objectives.

- Cost Management: Disciplined cost management is essential for driving profitability and maintaining financial stability. Leaders should implement strategies to optimize operational efficiency, control expenses, and maximize resource utilization.

- Investment in Innovation: Strategic investments in innovation are critical for sustaining long-term growth and competitiveness. Leaders should prioritize investments in research and development, technology, and talent to drive innovation and deliver value to customers.

- Prudent Risk Management: Effective financial management requires prudent risk management. Leaders should identify and mitigate financial risks, ensure regulatory compliance, and maintain a strong balance sheet to navigate economic uncertainties.

- Value Creation: Strategic acquisitions and capital allocation should be driven by a focus on value creation. Leaders should identify opportunities that enhance the company's competitive position, realize synergies, and deliver value to shareholders.

Safra Catz's impact on Oracle Corporation and the broader technology industry is a testament to her exceptional leadership, strategic vision, and financial acumen. Her contributions have transformed Oracle into a global technology powerhouse, driving innovation, expanding market reach, and delivering consistent financial performance.

Catz's strategic leadership has been characterized by her ability to articulate a clear vision, adapt to industry changes, and prioritize customer-centric solutions. Her financial acumen has been instrumental in achieving Oracle's financial goals, managing acquisitions, and optimizing capital allocation.

The lessons learned from Catz's leadership journey offer valuable insights for aspiring leaders and business professionals. By embracing strategic leadership, fostering a culture of innovation, and demonstrating financial acumen, leaders can drive sustainable growth, create value, and make a positive impact on their organizations and industries.

Safra Catz's legacy as a tech leader and visionary continues to inspire and influence future generations of business leaders. Her story is a powerful example of the impact that strategic vision, financial expertise, and unwavering determination can have on the success and transformation of a global enterprise.

Chapter 12: Lisa Su - The Semiconductor Pioneer

Lisa Su's journey to becoming a pivotal figure in the semiconductor industry is a remarkable story of talent, perseverance, and visionary leadership. Born on November 7, 1969, in Tainan, Taiwan, Su moved to the United States at the age of two with her family. Raised in Queens, New York, she grew up in an environment that valued education and hard work. Her parents, both academically inclined, encouraged her to pursue her interests and excel in her studies.

Early Education and Interests

Lisa Su demonstrated an early aptitude for science and mathematics. By the age of ten, she was already interested in engineering, a field traditionally dominated by men. Her parents supported her curiosity, providing her with her first personal computer, which she eagerly dismantled to understand its inner workings. This hands-on approach to learning fostered her passion for technology and engineering.

Su attended the Bronx High School of Science, a school known for its rigorous academic standards and focus on STEM education. Her outstanding performance in high school led her to the Massachusetts Institute of Technology (MIT), where she pursued a degree in Electrical Engineering. Su earned her bachelor's degree in 1990, followed by a master's degree in 1991, and a Ph.D. in Electrical

Engineering in 1994. Her doctoral research focused on semiconductor devices, specifically silicon-on-insulator (SOI) technology, which laid the foundation for her future career in the semiconductor industry.

Early Career in Semiconductor Technology

After completing her Ph.D., Lisa Su joined Texas Instruments as a member of the technical staff. At Texas Instruments, she worked on device physics and semiconductor research, gaining valuable experience in the field. In 1995, she moved to IBM, where she would spend the next 13 years of her career. IBM played a significant role in shaping her professional growth and expertise.

IBM: A Crucial Training Ground

At IBM, Su quickly distinguished herself through her innovative research and leadership abilities. She worked on a variety of projects related to semiconductor process technology and device fabrication. One of her notable contributions at IBM was her work on copper interconnect technology, which replaced aluminum in semiconductor devices, enhancing their performance and reliability. This breakthrough was a significant advancement in the field of semiconductor manufacturing.

Su's leadership potential was recognized early on, and she rose through the ranks at IBM, eventually becoming the Vice President of the Semiconductor Research and Development Center. In this role, she was responsible for IBM's semiconductor research efforts, managing a team of over 1,000 engineers and scientists. Her leadership and technical expertise were instrumental in driving innovations in semiconductor technology at IBM.

Transition to AMD

In 2012, Lisa Su made a significant career move by joining Advanced Micro Devices (AMD) as Senior Vice President and General Manager of Global Business Units. AMD, a company known for its microprocessors and graphics cards, was facing significant challenges at the time. The company was struggling with declining market share, financial losses, and stiff competition from industry giants like Intel and NVIDIA.

Su's decision to join AMD was driven by her belief in the company's potential and her desire to take on a new challenge. Her extensive experience in semiconductor technology and her leadership skills made her a valuable asset to AMD. She quickly took on key responsibilities, overseeing the company's global business operations and product development.

Achievements: Leading AMD as CEO and Transforming Its Fortunes

Lisa Su's leadership at AMD has been transformative. Since becoming CEO in October 2014, she has orchestrated a remarkable turnaround, revitalizing the company and positioning it as a formidable competitor in the semiconductor industry.

Strategic Vision and Leadership

Su's strategic vision and leadership have been central to AMD's resurgence. She recognized that for AMD to compete effectively, it needed to focus on innovation, product differentiation, and operational excellence.

- Focus on High-Performance Computing: One of Su's key strategic initiatives was to pivot AMD towards high-performance computing. She believed that AMD's strengths lay in developing high-performance CPUs and GPUs that could compete with Intel and NVIDIA. This focus on high-performance computing guided AMD's product development and marketing strategies.

- Investment in Research and Development: Under Su's leadership, AMD significantly increased its investment in research and development (R&D). She understood that innovation was critical to staying competitive in the fast-paced semiconductor industry. By prioritizing R&D, AMD was able to develop cutting-edge technologies and bring new, high-performance products to market.

- Operational Efficiency: Su also focused on improving AMD's operational efficiency. She streamlined the company's operations, reduced costs, and optimized its supply chain. These efforts helped improve AMD's financial performance and ensured that the company could deliver products to market more effectively.

Transformative Products and Technologies

Su's leadership has resulted in the development and launch of several transformative products and technologies that have redefined AMD's position in the market.

- Ryzen Processors: One of the most significant achievements under Su's leadership has been the development and launch of the Ryzen line of processors. Introduced in 2017, Ryzen processors are based on AMD's new Zen architecture, which offers significant performance improvements over previous generations. Ryzen processors have been highly competitive with Intel's offerings, gaining market share in both consumer and enterprise segments. The success of Ryzen has been a key driver of AMD's financial turnaround.

- EPYC Server Processors: In addition to Ryzen, AMD's EPYC server processors have also been a game-changer. Launched in 2017, EPYC processors are designed for data centers and enterprise applications. They offer superior performance, scalability, and energy efficiency, making them an attractive option for cloud service providers and enterprise customers. EPYC processors have helped AMD gain a foothold in the lucrative server market, challenging Intel's dominance.

- Radeon Graphics Cards: Under Su's leadership, AMD has also made significant strides in the graphics card market with its Radeon line of GPUs. Radeon GPUs, based on the RDNA architecture, offer competitive performance and efficiency, making them popular among gamers and professional users. The success of Radeon GPUs has strengthened AMD's position in the graphics card market and provided an alternative to NVIDIA's offerings.

Financial Turnaround and Market Performance

Lisa Su's strategic initiatives and leadership have resulted in a remarkable financial turnaround for AMD. The company's improved product portfolio and operational efficiency have translated into significant financial gains.

- Revenue Growth: Under Su's leadership, AMD's revenue has seen substantial growth. The company's annual revenue increased from $5.25 billion in 2014 to over $16 billion in 2021. This growth has been driven by strong demand for AMD's processors and graphics cards across various market segments.

- Profitability: AMD's profitability has also improved significantly under Su's leadership. The company transitioned from years of financial losses to achieving consistent profitability. This financial stability has allowed AMD to reinvest in R&D, further fueling its innovation and growth.

- Stock Performance: AMD's stock performance

has mirrored the company's financial turnaround. Since Su took over as CEO, AMD's stock price has increased dramatically, providing substantial returns for shareholders. The company's market capitalization has grown from around $2 billion in 2014 to over $150 billion in 2021, reflecting investor confidence in Su's leadership and AMD's future prospects.

Recognition and Awards

Lisa Su's achievements have garnered widespread recognition and numerous awards, highlighting her contributions to the semiconductor industry and her exceptional leadership.

- Barron's World's Best CEOs: Su has been named one of Barron's World's Best CEOs multiple times, reflecting her impact on AMD and her standing as a top business leader.

- Fortune's Most Powerful Women: Su has consistently been included in Fortune's Most Powerful Women list, recognizing her influence and leadership in the technology industry.

- IEEE Robert N. Noyce Medal: In 2021, Su was awarded the IEEE Robert N. Noyce Medal, one of the highest honors in the semiconductor industry. This award recognizes her outstanding contributions to the field of microelectronics and her leadership at AMD.

Challenges and Resilience

Su's journey at AMD has not been without challenges. The semiconductor industry is highly competitive, and AMD has faced significant hurdles along the way. However, Su's resilience and determination have been key factors in overcoming these challenges.

- Competitive Pressure: AMD operates in a highly competitive market, with formidable rivals like Intel and NVIDIA. Su's strategic focus on innovation and high-performance computing has enabled AMD to compete effectively and gain market share.

- Supply Chain Issues: The semiconductor industry has experienced supply chain disruptions and shortages, impacting production and delivery. Su's leadership in optimizing AMD's supply chain and managing relationships with suppliers has helped mitigate these challenges.

- Technological Advancements: Keeping pace with rapid technological advancements is a constant challenge in the semiconductor industry. Su's emphasis on R&D and her ability to anticipate industry trends have ensured that AMD remains at the forefront of innovation.

Vision for the Future

Lisa Su's vision for AMD's future is centered on continued innovation, market expansion, and leveraging emerging technologies. Her strategic priorities include:

- Advancing Semiconductor Technology: Su is committed to advancing semiconductor technology and pushing the boundaries of performance and efficiency. This includes ongoing development of AMD's CPU and GPU architectures, as well as exploring new areas such as artificial intelligence and machine learning.

- Expanding Market Presence: Su aims to expand AMD's market presence in key segments, including data centers, gaming, and professional graphics. By delivering competitive and innovative products, AMD seeks to capture a larger share of these growing markets.

- Sustainability and Corporate Responsibility: Su emphasizes the importance of sustainability and corporate responsibility. AMD is focused on reducing its environmental impact, promoting energy efficiency, and adopting sustainable business practices. Su's commitment to corporate responsibility extends to fostering diversity and inclusion within the company and the broader technology industry.

Lisa Su's journey in the technology sector and her transformative leadership at AMD exemplify the power of strategic vision, innovation, and resilience. Her contributions have not only revitalized AMD but also made a significant impact on the semiconductor industry as a whole.

Su's biography highlights her rise from a talented young engineer to a pioneering CEO, driven by a passion for technology and a commitment to excellence. Her achievements at AMD, including the development of groundbreaking products like Ryzen, EPYC, and Radeon, demonstrate her ability to drive innovation and compete in a highly competitive market.

Under Su's leadership, AMD has achieved remarkable financial success, gaining market share and delivering substantial returns to shareholders. Her strategic focus on high-performance computing, investment in R&D, and operational efficiency have positioned AMD as a formidable player in the semiconductor industry.

Lisa Su's story offers valuable lessons in leadership, strategic vision, and financial acumen. Her journey is an inspiration for aspiring leaders and professionals, showcasing the potential for transformative impact through dedication, innovation, and resilience. As AMD continues to evolve and thrive under her leadership, Lisa Su's legacy as a semiconductor pioneer and visionary leader will continue to inspire and influence the technology industry for years to come.

Impact on Industry: Shaping the Future of Semiconductors and Computing

Lisa Su's leadership at AMD has significantly shaped the semiconductor industry, influencing its trajectory and pushing the boundaries of what is possible in computing. Through her visionary leadership, AMD has not only revitalized its own fortunes but also driven innovations that have set new industry standards and opened up new possibilities for the future of semiconductors and computing.

Pioneering High-Performance Computing

Under Su's leadership, AMD has been at the forefront of high-performance computing (HPC), developing technologies and products that deliver exceptional performance and efficiency. This focus on HPC has had a profound impact on various industries, from gaming and entertainment to scientific research and artificial intelligence.

- Ryzen Processors: The introduction of AMD's Ryzen processors marked a significant advancement in CPU technology. Built on the Zen architecture, Ryzen processors offer superior performance, energy efficiency, and multi-threading capabilities. These processors have been widely adopted in both consumer and enterprise markets, driving innovations in gaming, content creation, and professional computing. The success of Ryzen has challenged Intel's dominance in the CPU market, leading to increased competition and accelerated technological advancements.

- EPYC Server Processors: AMD's EPYC server processors have revolutionized the data center and enterprise computing markets. EPYC processors provide unmatched performance, scalability, and energy efficiency, making them ideal for data-intensive applications such as cloud computing, big data analytics, and machine learning. The adoption of EPYC processors by major cloud service providers and enterprises has not only boosted AMD's market share but also set new benchmarks for server performance and efficiency.

- Radeon Graphics Cards: AMD's Radeon graphics cards, based on the RDNA architecture, have pushed the envelope in GPU technology. These graphics cards offer exceptional performance, power efficiency, and advanced features such as ray tracing and variable rate shading. Radeon GPUs have gained popularity among gamers, professionals, and content creators, driving innovations in gaming graphics, virtual reality, and digital content production.

Advancements in Semiconductor Technology

Lisa Su's leadership has also driven significant advancements in semiconductor technology, contributing to the evolution of the industry and setting new standards for innovation.

- 7nm and Beyond: Under Su's guidance, AMD was one of the first companies to adopt the 7nm process technology for its CPUs and GPUs. This transition to smaller process nodes has enabled AMD to deliver higher performance, lower power consumption, and greater transistor density. The successful implementation of 7nm technology has positioned AMD as a leader in semiconductor manufacturing, paving the way for future advancements in process technology.

- Chiplet Architecture: AMD's innovative chiplet architecture has redefined CPU design, enabling greater scalability and flexibility. By using multiple smaller chiplets interconnected on a single package, AMD has been able to improve manufacturing yields, reduce costs, and enhance performance. This approach has been particularly beneficial for high-core-count processors such as EPYC, providing a competitive edge in the data center market.

- Infinity Fabric: AMD's Infinity Fabric is a high-speed interconnect technology that enables efficient communication between different components within a processor. This innovation has been critical in achieving seamless integration of multiple chiplets and improving overall system performance. Infinity Fabric has also facilitated the development of AMD's APUs (Accelerated Processing Units), which combine CPU and GPU cores on a single chip, offering powerful and energy-efficient computing solutions.

Impact on Industry Standards and Practices

Lisa Su's leadership has influenced industry standards and practices, driving a shift towards more open and collaborative approaches to semiconductor development.

- Open Standards and Ecosystems: AMD has been a strong advocate for open standards and ecosystems, promoting interoperability and collaboration across the industry. This approach has enabled greater innovation and flexibility, allowing developers and customers to leverage AMD's technologies in a variety of applications. Initiatives such as the open-source ROCm (Radeon Open Compute) platform and support for industry standards like PCIe and HBM have reinforced AMD's commitment to open ecosystems.

- Collaboration with Industry Partners: Su has emphasized the importance of strategic partnerships and collaborations in driving innovation and growth. AMD has established strong relationships with key industry players, including Microsoft, Sony, Google, and major cloud service providers. These collaborations have facilitated the development and deployment of AMD's technologies in a wide range of products and services, from gaming consoles and laptops to cloud infrastructure and AI solutions.

- Influence on Competitors: AMD's resurgence under Su's leadership has had a significant impact on its competitors, particularly Intel and NVIDIA. The success of Ryzen, EPYC, and Radeon products has intensified competition in the CPU and GPU markets, prompting competitors to accelerate their own innovation efforts. This increased competition has benefited the industry as a whole, leading to faster advancements in technology and better products for consumers.

Driving Innovation in Computing

Lisa Su's leadership has not only transformed AMD but also driven broader innovations in computing, influencing the direction of the industry and shaping the future of technology.

- Artificial Intelligence and Machine Learning: AMD has made significant strides in artificial intelligence (AI) and machine learning (ML) under Su's leadership. The company's GPUs and APUs are optimized for AI and ML workloads, offering high-performance and energy-efficient solutions for training and inference. AMD's innovations in AI have enabled advancements in areas such as autonomous vehicles, natural language processing, and predictive analytics, driving the next wave of technological breakthroughs.

- High-Performance Computing for Research: AMD's high-performance computing solutions have played a crucial role in advancing scientific research and discovery. EPYC processors and Radeon GPUs are used in supercomputers and research institutions around the world, powering simulations, data analysis, and complex computations. These technologies have enabled breakthroughs in fields such as climate modeling, genomics, and astrophysics, contributing to our understanding of the world and the universe.

- Edge Computing and IoT: AMD's innovations in low-power, high-performance computing have also driven advancements in edge computing and the Internet of Things (IoT). AMD's embedded processors and APUs provide powerful and energy-efficient solutions for edge devices and IoT applications, enabling real-time data processing and analysis at the edge of the network. This has facilitated the development of smart cities, industrial automation, and connected healthcare, transforming how we live and work.

Lessons Learned: Innovation and Resilience in Technology

Lisa Su's leadership at AMD offers valuable lessons in embracing innovation and fostering a culture of continuous improvement. Her strategic focus on innovation has been instrumental in driving AMD's success and positioning the company as a leader in the semiconductor industry.

Fostering a Culture of Innovation

- Encouraging Creativity and Experimentation: Su has cultivated a culture of innovation at AMD by encouraging creativity and experimentation. She has empowered teams to explore new ideas, take calculated risks, and push the boundaries of technology. This culture of innovation has resulted in groundbreaking products and technologies that have redefined industry standards.

- Investing in Research and Development: Su's commitment to innovation is reflected in AMD's substantial investment in research and development (R&D). By prioritizing R&D, AMD has been able to stay ahead of industry trends and develop cutting-edge solutions that meet the evolving needs of customers. This focus on innovation has been critical in maintaining AMD's competitive edge and driving long-term growth.

- Collaborating with External Partners: Su recognizes the value of collaboration in driving innovation. AMD has established partnerships with academic institutions, research organizations, and industry leaders to leverage external expertise and resources. These collaborations have facilitated the development of new technologies and accelerated the commercialization of innovative solutions.

Strategic Vision for Innovation

- Anticipating Industry Trends: Su's strategic vision has been instrumental in guiding AMD's innovation efforts. She has a keen ability to anticipate industry trends and identify emerging opportunities. This foresight has enabled AMD to develop products and technologies that address future market demands and position the company for sustained success.

- Balancing Core Competencies and New Ventures: Su has struck a balance between leveraging AMD's core competencies and exploring new ventures. While maintaining a strong focus on high-performance computing and semiconductors, AMD has also ventured into new areas such as AI, machine learning, and edge computing. This balanced approach has diversified AMD's product portfolio and expanded its market reach.

- Driving Customer-Centric Innovation: Su's customer-centric approach has driven AMD's innovation strategy. By understanding and addressing the needs of customers, AMD has developed solutions that provide real value and meet market demands. This customer focus has strengthened AMD's relationships with key customers and partners, driving loyalty and business growth.

Demonstrating Resilience

Lisa Su's journey at AMD is also a powerful testament to resilience in the face of challenges. Her ability to navigate obstacles, adapt to changing circumstances, and persevere through difficult times has been a key factor in AMD's success.

Navigating Industry Challenges

- Overcoming Financial Difficulties: When Su joined AMD, the company was facing significant financial challenges, including declining market share and mounting losses. Her strategic initiatives and leadership have been instrumental in turning AMD's fortunes around. By focusing on innovation, operational efficiency, and market expansion, Su has restored AMD's financial stability and driven consistent growth.

- Competing with Industry Giants: AMD operates in a highly competitive industry, with formidable rivals such as Intel and NVIDIA. Su's resilience and determination have enabled AMD to compete effectively and gain market share. Her strategic focus on high-performance computing and differentiated products has positioned AMD as a strong competitor in the CPU and GPU markets.

- Adapting to Technological Advancements: The semiconductor industry is characterized by rapid technological advancements and evolving market demands. Su's ability to adapt to these changes and guide AMD through periods of transition has been critical to the company's success. Her focus on continuous innovation and strategic investments has ensured that AMD remains at the forefront of technological advancements.

Building a Resilient Organization

- Empowering Teams: Su has built a resilient organization by empowering teams and fostering a culture of collaboration and accountability. She has created an environment where employees are encouraged to take ownership of their work, contribute their ideas, and work together to achieve common goals.

This collaborative culture has strengthened AMD's ability to navigate challenges and seize opportunities.

- Maintaining Operational Agility: Su's leadership has also emphasized the importance of operational agility. By streamlining operations, optimizing processes, and enhancing supply chain management, AMD has become more agile and responsive to market changes. This operational agility has enabled AMD to quickly adapt to disruptions and maintain business continuity.

- Cultivating a Growth Mindset: Su has instilled a growth mindset within AMD, encouraging continuous learning, development, and improvement. This growth mindset has driven employees to embrace challenges, learn from failures, and strive for excellence. By fostering a culture of resilience and continuous improvement, Su has positioned AMD for sustained success.

Lessons in Innovation and Resilience

Lisa Su's leadership journey offers valuable lessons in innovation and resilience for aspiring leaders and professionals.

- Embrace a Culture of Innovation: Leaders should cultivate a culture of innovation by encouraging creativity, experimentation, and risk-taking. By empowering teams to explore new ideas and push the boundaries of technology, organizations can drive continuous innovation and stay ahead of industry trends.

- Invest in Research and Development: Strategic investments in research and development are critical for driving innovation and maintaining a competitive edge. Leaders should prioritize R&D and allocate resources to develop cutting-edge technologies and solutions that meet market demands.

- Collaborate and Leverage External Expertise: Collaboration with external partners, academic institutions, and research organizations can enhance innovation efforts and accelerate the commercialization of new technologies. Leaders should seek strategic partnerships to leverage external expertise and resources.

- Demonstrate Resilience in the Face of Challenges: Resilience is essential for navigating industry challenges and achieving long-term success. Leaders should demonstrate resilience by adapting to changing circumstances, persevering through difficult times, and maintaining a strategic focus on long-term goals.

- Build a Resilient Organization: Empowering teams, fostering collaboration, and maintaining operational agility are key to building a resilient organization. Leaders should create an environment that encourages ownership, accountability, and continuous improvement, positioning the organization for sustained success.

Lisa Su's impact on the semiconductor industry and her transformative leadership at AMD have shaped the future of semiconductors and computing. Her strategic vision, focus on innovation, and resilience have driven AMD's success and positioned the company as a leader in high-performance computing and semiconductor technology.

Under Su's leadership, AMD has developed groundbreaking products such as Ryzen processors, EPYC server processors, and Radeon graphics cards, redefining industry standards and driving technological advancements. Her commitment to innovation and customer-centric solutions has strengthened AMD's competitive position and expanded its market reach.

Su's journey offers valuable lessons in innovation and resilience, emphasizing the importance of fostering a culture of innovation, investing in research and development, and demonstrating resilience in the face of challenges. Her leadership has not only transformed AMD but also influenced the broader semiconductor industry, driving advancements in computing and shaping the future of technology.

As AMD continues to evolve and thrive under Lisa Su's leadership, her legacy as a semiconductor pioneer and visionary leader will continue to inspire and influence future generations of business leaders and technology professionals. Her story is a powerful example of the impact that strategic vision, innovation, and resilience can have on the success and transformation of a global enterprise.

Chapter 13: Rosalind Brewer - The Retail Trailblazer

Rosalind "Roz" Brewer has become one of the most influential figures in the retail industry, known for her strategic vision, leadership prowess, and commitment to diversity and inclusion. Born on August 19, 1962, in Detroit, Michigan, Brewer's journey to the top of the retail world is a story of perseverance, talent, and groundbreaking achievements.

Early Life and Education

Brewer grew up in a family that valued education and hard work. Her parents emphasized the importance of academic achievement and instilled in her a strong work ethic. Brewer attended Cass Technical High School in Detroit, where she excelled in her studies and demonstrated an early interest in science and mathematics.

She pursued her undergraduate education at Spelman College, a historically black liberal arts college for women in Atlanta, Georgia. Brewer graduated in 1984 with a degree in chemistry. During her time at Spelman, she also became a member of the Alpha Kappa Alpha sorority, which reinforced her commitment to service and leadership. Her education at Spelman laid a strong foundation for her analytical skills and critical thinking, which would prove invaluable in her future career.

Early Career and Entry into Retail

After graduating from Spelman College, Brewer began her career in the pharmaceutical industry. She joined Kimberly-Clark Corporation, a global health and hygiene company, where she worked for 22 years. Brewer held various leadership positions at Kimberly-Clark, including roles in manufacturing and product development. Her experience at Kimberly-Clark provided her with a solid understanding of business operations, supply chain management, and product innovation.

Brewer's transition to the retail industry came in 2006 when she joined Walmart. She initially served as the Regional Vice President overseeing operations in Georgia. Her leadership and performance in this role quickly earned her a promotion to President of Walmart's Southeast market, where she was responsible for a significant portion of Walmart's business in the United States.

Rise at Walmart

Brewer's success continued at Walmart, where she took on increasingly senior roles. In 2012, she was appointed President and CEO of Sam's Club, a membership-only retail warehouse club and a division of Walmart. This appointment made her the first African American to lead a Walmart division and one of the highest-ranking African American executives in the retail industry.

As CEO of Sam's Club, Brewer implemented several strategic initiatives to drive growth and improve the customer experience. She focused on enhancing the quality of products, expanding the company's e-commerce capabilities, and leveraging data analytics to better understand customer preferences. Brewer also championed efforts to improve diversity and inclusion within the organization.

Joining Starbucks

In 2017, Brewer made another significant career move by joining Starbucks as Chief Operating Officer (COO) and Group President. At Starbucks, she was responsible for overseeing the company's operations in the Americas, which included the United States, Canada, and Latin America. Brewer's role at Starbucks was pivotal in driving the company's growth and operational excellence.

Leadership at Starbucks

As COO of Starbucks, Brewer played a crucial role in leading the company's global operations and strategic initiatives. She focused on enhancing the customer experience, expanding Starbucks' digital capabilities, and driving growth in key markets.

- Customer Experience: Brewer emphasized the importance of creating a welcoming and inclusive environment for customers. She implemented initiatives to improve the quality of service, streamline operations, and enhance the overall customer experience. Her efforts contributed to increased customer satisfaction and loyalty.

- Digital Transformation: Brewer was instrumental in driving Starbucks' digital transformation. She oversaw the expansion of the company's mobile ordering and payment systems, which significantly improved convenience for customers. Brewer also led efforts to leverage data analytics to personalize customer interactions and optimize operations.

- Growth and Expansion: Brewer played a key role in expanding Starbucks' presence in key markets, including the United States, Canada, and Latin America. She focused on identifying growth opportunities, optimizing store operations, and expanding the company's product offerings. Brewer's strategic initiatives helped drive revenue growth and strengthen Starbucks' market position.

Appointment as CEO of Walgreens Boots Alliance

In March 2021, Brewer was appointed CEO of Walgreens Boots Alliance (WBA), becoming the first African American woman to lead a Fortune 500 company. This appointment marked a significant milestone in her career and highlighted her exceptional leadership capabilities.

As CEO of WBA, Brewer has been responsible for leading the company's global operations and strategic initiatives. Her vision for WBA includes enhancing the customer experience, expanding healthcare services, and driving operational excellence. Brewer's leadership at WBA has been characterized by her focus on innovation, digital transformation, and commitment to diversity and inclusion.

Achievements: Leading as CEO of Walgreens Boots Alliance and Starbucks COO

Transformative Leadership at Starbucks

Brewer's tenure as COO of Starbucks was marked by several significant achievements that transformed the company and positioned it for continued growth and success.

Enhancing Customer Experience

- Operational Excellence: Brewer implemented initiatives to streamline operations and improve efficiency across Starbucks' stores. She focused on optimizing store layouts, improving inventory management, and enhancing the quality of service. These efforts resulted in a more consistent and satisfying customer experience, contributing to increased customer loyalty and sales.

- Inclusive Environment: Brewer championed efforts to create a more inclusive and welcoming environment for customers. She introduced training programs for employees to promote diversity, equity, and inclusion. These initiatives helped foster a culture of respect and inclusion within Starbucks stores, enhancing the overall customer experience.

- Store Formats: Brewer led the development

and expansion of new store formats, including Starbucks Reserve and Starbucks Roastery locations. These premium store formats offered unique and immersive experiences for customers, showcasing Starbucks' commitment to quality and innovation.

Driving Digital Transformation

- Mobile Ordering and Payment: Brewer was instrumental in expanding Starbucks' mobile ordering and payment capabilities. Under her leadership, Starbucks enhanced its mobile app, allowing customers to order and pay for their beverages and food items ahead of time. This innovation significantly improved convenience for customers and contributed to increased sales and customer engagement.

- Personalization and Data Analytics: Brewer leveraged data analytics to personalize customer interactions and optimize operations. By analyzing customer data, Starbucks was able to offer personalized recommendations and promotions, enhancing the overall customer experience. Brewer's focus on data-driven decision-making helped drive revenue growth and operational efficiency.

- Loyalty Program: Brewer played a key role in expanding Starbucks' loyalty program, Starbucks Rewards. The program offered customers rewards and incentives for their purchases, encouraging repeat business and increasing customer loyalty. The success of the loyalty program contributed to Starbucks' revenue growth and market share.

- Growth and Expansion

- Market Expansion: Brewer focused on expanding Starbucks' presence in key markets, including the United States, Canada, and Latin America. She identified growth opportunities and implemented strategies to optimize store operations and drive revenue growth. Under her leadership, Starbucks opened new stores in high-growth markets, strengthening its market position.

- Product Innovation: Brewer led efforts to expand Starbucks' product offerings, introducing new beverages, food items, and merchandise. These innovations helped attract new customers and drive sales growth. Brewer's focus on product innovation ensured that Starbucks remained relevant and competitive in the ever-evolving retail landscape.

- Sustainability Initiatives: Brewer championed sustainability initiatives at Starbucks, emphasizing the importance of environmental responsibility. She led efforts to reduce waste, promote recycling, and source sustainable ingredients. These initiatives aligned with Starbucks' commitment to corporate social responsibility and resonated with environmentally conscious customers.

Transformative Leadership at Walgreens Boots Alliance

Brewer's appointment as CEO of Walgreens Boots Alliance marked a new chapter in her career and brought her transformative leadership to the healthcare and retail sectors.

Enhancing Healthcare Services

- Healthcare Integration: Brewer's vision for WBA includes expanding the company's healthcare services and integrating them with its retail operations. She has focused on enhancing the accessibility and affordability of healthcare for customers, positioning WBA as a leader in the healthcare retail space.

- Pharmacy Services: Brewer has led initiatives to expand and improve WBA's pharmacy services. This includes increasing the availability of prescription medications, offering immunization services, and providing personalized health consultations. Brewer's focus on pharmacy services has helped WBA meet the evolving healthcare needs of its customers.

- Health and Wellness Products: Brewer has driven efforts to expand WBA's range of health and wellness products. This includes offering a wider selection of vitamins, supplements, and over-the-counter medications. Brewer's commitment to health and wellness has strengthened WBA's position as a trusted provider of healthcare products.

Driving Digital Transformation

- Digital Health Platforms: Brewer has championed the development of digital health platforms at WBA. This includes expanding telehealth services, enabling customers to access healthcare professionals remotely. Brewer's focus on digital health has improved the convenience and accessibility of healthcare for customers.

- E-Commerce and Online Services: Brewer has led efforts to enhance WBA's e-commerce capabilities and online services. This includes improving the company's website and mobile app, allowing customers to order products online and have them delivered to their homes or pick them up in-store. Brewer's focus on digital transformation has driven revenue growth and improved the customer experience.

- Data-Driven Decision Making: Brewer has leveraged data analytics to inform strategic decisions and optimize operations at WBA. By analyzing customer data, WBA has been able to offer personalized recommendations and promotions, enhancing the overall customer experience. Brewer's focus on data-driven decision-making has improved operational efficiency and customer satisfaction.

Commitment to Diversity and Inclusion

- Diversity Initiatives: Brewer has championed diversity and inclusion initiatives at WBA, emphasizing the importance of creating a diverse and inclusive workplace. She has implemented programs to promote diversity in hiring, leadership development, and supplier diversity. Brewer's commitment to diversity has helped foster a more inclusive culture at WBA.

- Equity and Inclusion Training: Brewer has introduced training programs to promote equity and inclusion within WBA. These programs aim to raise awareness of unconscious bias, promote respectful communication, and create a more inclusive environment. Brewer's focus on equity and inclusion has strengthened WBA's organizational culture and employee engagement.

- Community Engagement: Brewer has led efforts to engage with and support the communities that WBA serves. This includes initiatives to address health disparities, promote health education, and provide resources to underserved communities. Brewer's commitment to community engagement has reinforced WBA's role as a responsible corporate citizen.

Financial Performance and Growth

Brewer's leadership has had a positive impact on WBA's financial performance and growth. Her strategic initiatives and focus on operational excellence have driven revenue growth and improved profitability.

- Revenue Growth: Under Brewer's leadership, WBA has achieved significant revenue growth. Her focus on expanding healthcare services, enhancing digital capabilities, and optimizing operations has contributed to increased sales and market share. Brewer's strategic vision has positioned WBA for sustained growth and success.

- Operational Efficiency: Brewer has implemented initiatives to improve operational efficiency at WBA. This includes streamlining processes, optimizing supply chain management, and reducing costs. Brewer's focus on operational efficiency has enhanced WBA's financial performance and competitiveness.

- Market Expansion: Brewer has driven efforts to expand WBA's presence in key markets. This includes opening new stores, acquiring strategic assets, and entering new markets. Brewer's focus on market expansion has strengthened WBA's market position and growth prospects.

Lessons Learned: Strategic Leadership and Financial Acumen

Rosalind Brewer's leadership journey offers valuable lessons in strategic leadership, particularly in the context of navigating the complex and dynamic retail and healthcare industries. Her ability to develop and execute a clear strategic vision has been instrumental in her success.

Visionary Leadership

- Articulating a Clear Vision: Brewer's ability to articulate a clear and compelling vision for WBA's future has been a cornerstone of her leadership. She has consistently communicated the company's strategic goals and priorities, ensuring that employees, stakeholders, and customers understand and are aligned with the company's direction. This clarity of vision has provided a sense of purpose and direction, motivating the organization to achieve its objectives.

- Long-Term Thinking: Brewer's strategic leadership is characterized by her focus on long-term thinking. She has emphasized the importance of investing in innovation, infrastructure, and talent to drive sustainable growth. By taking a long-term perspective, Brewer has ensured that WBA remains resilient and competitive in a rapidly changing industry.

Adaptability and Resilience

- Navigating Industry Changes: The retail and healthcare industries are characterized by rapid innovation and change. Brewer's ability to adapt to these changes and position WBA for continued success has been a key factor in her leadership. She has demonstrated a willingness to pivot strategies, embrace new technologies, and explore emerging markets. This adaptability has enabled WBA to stay ahead of industry trends and seize new opportunities.

- Resilience in the Face of Challenges: Brewer's resilience in the face of challenges has been evident throughout her tenure at WBA. She has navigated complex mergers and acquisitions, regulatory scrutiny, and economic uncertainties with confidence and determination. Her resilience has inspired confidence within the organization and has helped WBA overcome obstacles and achieve its strategic goals.

Innovation and Customer-Centric Solutions

- Fostering a Culture of Innovation: Brewer has championed a culture of innovation at WBA, encouraging employees to think creatively and develop cutting-edge solutions. She has supported investments in research and development, ensuring that WBA remains at the forefront of technological advancements. This focus on innovation has enabled WBA to deliver products and services that meet the evolving needs of its customers.

- Customer-Centric Approach: Brewer's strategic leadership has been characterized by a customer-centric approach. She has emphasized the importance of understanding and addressing customer needs, developing solutions that provide real value. By prioritizing customer satisfaction and building strong relationships, Brewer has strengthened WBA's brand and competitive position.

Financial Acumen

Rosalind Brewer's financial acumen has been a driving force behind WBA's financial success and stability. Her expertise in corporate finance, strategic planning, and financial management has been instrumental in achieving the company's financial goals.

Financial Stewardship

- Effective Financial Management: Brewer's role as CEO has involved overseeing WBA's financial strategy and performance. She has demonstrated effective financial management, ensuring that the company maintains a strong balance sheet, generates consistent revenue growth, and delivers value to shareholders. Her financial stewardship has been characterized by disciplined cost management, strategic investments, and prudent risk management.

- Driving Profitability: Under Brewer's

leadership, WBA's profitability has improved significantly. She has implemented strategies to drive profitability, including optimizing operational efficiency, streamlining processes, and leveraging economies of scale. Brewer's focus on profitability has enabled WBA to reinvest in innovation and growth initiatives.

Strategic Acquisitions

- Value-Driven Acquisitions: Brewer's approach to acquisitions has been driven by a focus on value creation. She has identified and pursued acquisitions that align with WBA's strategic goals, enhance its product portfolio, and expand its market reach. By integrating acquired companies effectively, Brewer has maximized the value of these acquisitions and strengthened WBA's competitive position.

- Synergy Realization: Brewer's financial acumen has been critical in realizing synergies from acquisitions. She has implemented strategies to integrate acquired companies, optimize resources, and achieve cost savings. This focus on synergy realization has enhanced the financial performance of acquired businesses and contributed to WBA's overall growth.

Capital Allocation

- Strategic Investments: Brewer's expertise in capital allocation has enabled WBA to make strategic investments in technology, infrastructure, and talent. She has prioritized investments that drive innovation, enhance operational efficiency, and support long-term growth. This strategic approach to capital allocation has ensured that WBA remains competitive and positioned for future success.

- Shareholder Value: Brewer's financial acumen has also been evident in her commitment to delivering value to shareholders. WBA has implemented share buyback programs and dividend policies that reflect the company's financial strength and commitment to returning capital to shareholders. These initiatives have enhanced shareholder value and demonstrated Brewer's focus on financial performance.

Lessons in Financial Acumen

Rosalind Brewer's financial acumen offers valuable lessons for business leaders and financial professionals.

- Strategic Planning: Effective financial management requires strategic planning and a clear understanding of the company's financial goals. Leaders should develop comprehensive financial strategies that align with the company's overall vision and objectives.

- Cost Management: Disciplined cost management is essential for driving profitability and maintaining financial stability. Leaders should implement strategies to optimize operational efficiency, control expenses, and maximize resource utilization.

- Investment in Innovation: Strategic investments in innovation are critical for sustaining long-term growth and competitiveness. Leaders should prioritize investments in research and development, technology, and talent to drive innovation and deliver value to customers.

- Prudent Risk Management: Effective financial management requires prudent risk management. Leaders should identify and mitigate financial risks, ensure regulatory compliance, and maintain a strong balance sheet to navigate economic uncertainties.

- Value Creation: Strategic acquisitions and capital allocation should be driven by a focus on value creation. Leaders should identify opportunities that enhance the company's competitive position, realize synergies, and deliver value to shareholders.

Rosalind Brewer's impact on the retail and healthcare industries and her transformative leadership at Walgreens Boots Alliance and Starbucks exemplify the power of strategic vision, innovation, and financial acumen. Her contributions have not only revitalized the companies she has led but also set new standards for diversity, inclusion, and corporate responsibility.

Brewer's biography highlights her rise from a talented young chemist to a trailblazing CEO, driven by a passion for excellence and a commitment to making a positive impact. Her achievements at Starbucks and WBA, including the development of groundbreaking initiatives and transformative strategies, demonstrate her ability to drive innovation and compete in highly competitive markets.

Under Brewer's leadership, WBA has achieved remarkable financial success, gaining market share and delivering substantial returns to shareholders. Her strategic focus on healthcare services, digital transformation, and operational efficiency has positioned WBA as a leader in the healthcare retail space.

Rosalind Brewer's story offers valuable lessons in strategic leadership, financial acumen, and resilience. Her journey is an inspiration for aspiring leaders and professionals, showcasing the potential for transformative impact through dedication, innovation, and resilience. As WBA continues to evolve and thrive under her leadership, Rosalind Brewer's legacy as a retail trailblazer and visionary leader will continue to inspire and influence the retail and healthcare industries for years to come.

Impact on Industry: Driving Innovation and Inclusion in Retail

Rosalind Brewer's tenure at companies like Sam's Club, Starbucks, and Walgreens Boots Alliance has been marked by a commitment to driving innovation in the retail sector. Her strategic vision and leadership have resulted in numerous transformative initiatives that have redefined customer experiences, optimized operations, and leveraged technology to stay ahead of industry trends.

Enhancing Customer Experience through Innovation

- Operational Excellence: At Sam's Club, Brewer focused on enhancing operational efficiency and the overall customer experience. She implemented several key initiatives aimed at streamlining store operations, improving inventory management, and optimizing supply chain processes. By leveraging data analytics and technology, Brewer was able to ensure that products were always in stock and available to members, thereby enhancing customer satisfaction and loyalty.

- Digital Transformation: Brewer recognized the importance of digital transformation in the retail industry. During her time at Starbucks, she spearheaded efforts to expand the company's mobile ordering and payment systems. This innovation significantly improved convenience for customers, allowing them to order and pay for their beverages and food items ahead of time. Brewer's focus on digital capabilities helped Starbucks stay competitive in an increasingly tech-driven marketplace.

- Personalization and Data Analytics: Brewer leveraged data analytics to personalize customer interactions and improve service quality. At Starbucks, she led initiatives to analyze customer data, which enabled the company to offer personalized recommendations and promotions. This focus on data-driven decision-making not only enhanced the customer experience but also drove sales growth by aligning product offerings with customer preferences.

- Store Formats and Experiences: Brewer introduced new store formats and experiences to attract different customer segments. Under her leadership, Starbucks developed and expanded its Reserve and Roastery locations, which offered premium coffee experiences and exclusive products. These upscale store formats provided unique and immersive experiences for customers, showcasing Starbucks' commitment to quality and innovation.

Driving Digital and E-Commerce Growth

- Mobile Ordering and Payment Systems: One of Brewer's most significant contributions to Starbucks was the expansion of its mobile ordering and payment systems. By enhancing the Starbucks mobile app, she made it easier for customers to order and pay for their purchases. This innovation led to a substantial increase in mobile orders, driving sales and improving operational efficiency in stores.

- E-Commerce Expansion: Brewer also played a key role in expanding Starbucks' e-commerce capabilities. She oversaw the enhancement of the company's online store, allowing customers to purchase a wide range of Starbucks products, including coffee, merchandise, and brewing equipment. Brewer's focus on e-commerce growth helped Starbucks reach a broader customer base and drive additional revenue streams.

- Digital Health Platforms: At Walgreens Boots Alliance, Brewer has continued to drive digital innovation. She has championed the development of digital health platforms, including telehealth services and online health consultations. These digital health initiatives have improved the accessibility and convenience of healthcare services for customers, positioning Walgreens as a leader in the digital health space.

Innovative Health and Wellness Solutions

- Integrated Healthcare Services: Brewer's vision for Walgreens Boots Alliance includes expanding the company's healthcare services and integrating them with its retail operations. Under her leadership, Walgreens has enhanced its pharmacy services, offering immunizations, health screenings, and personalized health consultations. This focus on integrated healthcare services has improved the overall customer experience and positioned Walgreens as a trusted healthcare provider.

- Health and Wellness Products: Brewer has driven efforts to expand Walgreens' range of health and wellness products. She has focused on offering a wide selection of vitamins, supplements, and over-the-counter medications, as well as promoting wellness programs and initiatives. Brewer's commitment to health and wellness has strengthened Walgreens' position as a leader in the health retail sector.

- Sustainability and Environmental Responsibility: Brewer has also emphasized the importance of sustainability and environmental responsibility in Walgreens' operations. She has led initiatives to reduce waste, promote recycling, and source sustainable products. These efforts align with Brewer's commitment to corporate social responsibility and resonate with environmentally conscious customers.

Impact on Industry Standards and Practices

Brewer's innovative leadership has influenced industry standards and practices, setting new benchmarks for excellence in retail and healthcare.

- Customer-Centric Innovation: Brewer's focus on customer-centric innovation has set a new standard for the retail industry. Her initiatives to enhance the customer experience, personalize interactions, and leverage digital technologies have been widely adopted by other retailers, driving industry-wide improvements in service quality and convenience.

- Digital Transformation: Brewer's leadership in

digital transformation has influenced the retail sector's approach to technology and innovation. Her success in expanding mobile ordering, e-commerce, and digital health platforms has demonstrated the importance of embracing technology to stay competitive and meet evolving customer needs.

- Integrated Healthcare Services: Brewer's vision for integrated healthcare services has set a new benchmark for the healthcare retail sector. Her efforts to expand pharmacy services and promote health and wellness have inspired other retailers to adopt similar strategies, improving the accessibility and quality of healthcare for consumers.

Lessons Learned: Strategic Leadership and Advocating for Diversity

Rosalind Brewer's career offers valuable lessons in strategic leadership, particularly in the context of navigating complex and dynamic industries. Her ability to develop and execute a clear strategic vision has been instrumental in driving innovation and achieving organizational success.

Visionary Leadership

- Articulating a Clear Vision: Brewer's ability to articulate a clear and compelling vision for her organizations has been a cornerstone of her leadership. She consistently communicates strategic goals and priorities, ensuring that employees, stakeholders, and customers are aligned with the company's direction. This clarity of vision provides a sense of purpose and motivation, driving the organization toward its objectives.

- Long-Term Thinking: Brewer's strategic leadership is characterized by her focus on long-term thinking. She emphasizes the importance of investing in innovation, infrastructure, and talent to drive sustainable growth. By taking a long-term perspective, Brewer ensures that her organizations remain resilient and competitive in rapidly changing industries.

Adaptability and Resilience

- Navigating Industry Changes: The retail and healthcare industries are characterized by rapid innovation and change. Brewer's ability to adapt to these changes and position her organizations for continued success has been a key factor in her leadership. She demonstrates a willingness to pivot strategies, embrace new technologies, and explore emerging markets. This adaptability enables her organizations to stay ahead of industry trends and seize new opportunities.

- Resilience in the Face of Challenges: Brewer's resilience in the face of challenges has been evident throughout her career. She navigates complex mergers and acquisitions, regulatory scrutiny, and economic uncertainties with confidence and determination. Her resilience inspires confidence within her organizations and helps them overcome obstacles and achieve strategic goals.

Innovation and Customer-Centric Solutions

- Fostering a Culture of Innovation: Brewer champions a culture of innovation by encouraging employees to think creatively and develop cutting-edge solutions. She supports investments in research and development, ensuring that her organizations remain at the forefront of technological advancements. This focus on innovation enables her organizations to deliver products and services that meet evolving customer needs.

- Customer-Centric Approach: Brewer's strategic leadership is characterized by a customer-centric approach. She emphasizes the importance of understanding and addressing customer needs, developing solutions that provide real value. By prioritizing customer satisfaction and building strong relationships, Brewer strengthens her organizations' brands and competitive positions.

Advocating for Diversity

Rosalind Brewer is a passionate advocate for diversity and inclusion, and her commitment to these principles has had a profound impact on the organizations she has led. Her efforts to promote diversity and inclusion have not only enhanced organizational culture but also driven business success.

Championing Diversity and Inclusion

- Diversity Initiatives: Brewer has championed diversity and inclusion initiatives at every organization she has led. She implements programs to promote diversity in hiring, leadership development, and supplier diversity. Brewer's commitment to diversity fosters a more inclusive culture and enhances the overall performance of her organizations.

- Equity and Inclusion Training: Brewer introduces training programs to promote equity and inclusion within her organizations. These programs raise awareness of unconscious bias, promote respectful communication, and create a more inclusive environment. Brewer's focus on equity and inclusion strengthens organizational culture and employee engagement.

- Mentorship and Support: Brewer is a strong advocate for mentorship and support, particularly for underrepresented groups. She mentors emerging leaders and provides guidance and support to help them navigate their careers. Brewer's commitment to mentorship helps develop diverse talent and fosters a more inclusive leadership pipeline.

Impact on Organizational Performance

Enhanced Creativity and Innovation: Promoting

diversity and inclusion enhances creativity and innovation within organizations. Diverse teams bring a wide range of perspectives and experiences, leading to more innovative solutions and better decision-making. Brewer's commitment to diversity has driven innovation and improved organizational performance.

- Improved Employee Engagement: Creating an inclusive environment improves employee engagement and satisfaction. Employees who feel valued and respected are more likely to be engaged, productive, and committed to their organizations. Brewer's focus on diversity and inclusion has strengthened employee engagement and retention.

- Stronger Customer Relationships: Promoting diversity and inclusion helps organizations build stronger relationships with their customers. By understanding and addressing the diverse needs of their customers, organizations can provide better products and services. Brewer's commitment to diversity has enhanced customer satisfaction and loyalty.

Lessons in Advocating for Diversity

Rosalind Brewer's advocacy for diversity offers valuable lessons for business leaders and professionals.

- Commitment to Diversity: Leaders should demonstrate a strong commitment to diversity and inclusion. This includes implementing diversity initiatives, promoting equity and inclusion, and fostering an inclusive culture. By prioritizing diversity, leaders can enhance organizational performance and drive business success.

- Inclusive Leadership: Inclusive leadership is essential for promoting diversity and inclusion. Leaders should create an environment where all employees feel valued, respected, and included. This includes providing mentorship and support, addressing unconscious bias, and promoting respectful communication.

- Leveraging Diversity for Innovation: Leaders should leverage diversity to drive innovation and creativity. Diverse teams bring a wide range of perspectives and experiences, leading to more innovative solutions and better decision-making. By promoting diversity, leaders can enhance their organizations' ability to innovate and compete in the marketplace.

- Building Strong Relationships: Promoting diversity and inclusion helps organizations build strong relationships with their employees, customers, and stakeholders. By understanding and addressing diverse needs, organizations can provide better products and services and build stronger connections with their communities.

Rosalind Brewer's impact on the retail and healthcare industries and her transformative leadership at Sam's Club, Starbucks, and Walgreens Boots Alliance exemplify the power of strategic vision, innovation, and advocacy for diversity. Her contributions have not only revitalized the companies she has led but also set new standards for excellence in retail and healthcare.

Brewer's commitment to driving innovation and enhancing the customer experience has resulted in numerous transformative initiatives that have redefined industry standards and practices. Her focus on digital transformation, e-commerce growth, and integrated healthcare services has positioned her organizations for continued success in rapidly changing industries.

Brewer's advocacy for diversity and inclusion has had a profound impact on organizational culture and performance. Her efforts to promote diversity, equity, and inclusion have enhanced creativity and innovation, improved employee engagement, and strengthened customer relationships. Brewer's leadership in diversity and inclusion serves as a powerful example for business leaders and professionals.

Rosalind Brewer's story offers valuable lessons in strategic leadership, innovation, and advocating for diversity. Her journey is an inspiration for aspiring leaders and professionals, showcasing the potential for transformative impact through dedication, innovation, and resilience. As Walgreens Boots Alliance continues to evolve and thrive under her leadership, Rosalind Brewer's legacy as a retail trailblazer and visionary leader will continue to inspire and influence the retail and healthcare industries for years to come.

Chapter 14: Conclusion - The Legacy of Female Business Leaders

Throughout the histories of Estee Lauder, Mary Kay Ash, Oprah Winfrey, Martha Stewart, Meg Whitman, Sara Blakely, Indra Nooyi, Angela Ahrendts, Sheila Johnson, Safra Catz, Lisa Su, and Rosalind Brewer, several key lessons emerge that highlight their paths to success and the lasting impact they have had on their respective industries.

Estee Lauder - The Beauty Mogul

- Personal Branding: Estee Lauder's focus on creating a personal connection with her customers and ensuring that her products were of the highest quality helped her build a lasting brand.

- Innovation: She pioneered techniques in marketing, such as free samples and beauty consultations, which have become industry standards.

Mary Kay Ash - The Direct Selling Pioneer

- Empowerment: Mary Kay Ash's focus on empowering her sales force by offering incentives and creating a supportive community led to the remarkable growth of her company.

- Networking: Building strong networks and relationships was key to her business model and success.

Oprah Winfrey - The Media Powerhouse

- Authenticity: Oprah's success was driven by her authentic connection with her audience and her willingness to share personal stories.

- Diversification: She expanded her brand beyond television into various media and business ventures, maintaining her influence across multiple platforms.

Martha Stewart - The Domestic Diva

- Diversification and Brand Consistency: Martha Stewart successfully expanded her brand across various media and product lines while maintaining a consistent brand image.

- Attention to Detail: Her meticulous attention to detail and high standards set her apart in the lifestyle industry.

Meg Whitman - The E-Commerce Innovator

- Strategic Vision: Meg Whitman's strategic vision for eBay transformed it from a small auction website into a global e-commerce giant.

- Adaptability: Her ability to adapt and lead in the rapidly changing tech environment was crucial to her success.

Sara Blakely - The Shapewear Visionary

- Innovation and Persistence: Blakely's innovative approach to creating shapewear and her persistence in bringing her product to market were key to her success.

- Direct Marketing: Using herself as the brand's spokesperson helped establish a personal connection with customers.

Indra Nooyi - The Corporate Strategist

- Strategic Leadership: Indra Nooyi's focus on strategic growth and sustainability drove PepsiCo's success.

- Corporate Responsibility: Her emphasis on corporate responsibility and health innovation helped align the company's business practices with emerging consumer values.

Angela Ahrendts - The Luxury Retail Leader

- Brand Revitalization: Ahrendts revitalized Burberry by integrating digital innovation with traditional retail practices.

- Customer Experience: She placed a strong emphasis on enhancing the customer experience, which drove brand loyalty and growth.

Sheila Johnson - The Media Magnate

- Diversification: Johnson's ability to diversify her business interests across media, sports, and hospitality exemplifies her entrepreneurial spirit.

- Social Impact: Her commitment to philanthropy and social causes highlights the importance of using business success to make a positive impact.

Safra Catz - The Tech Leader

- Financial Acumen: Catz's financial expertise was crucial in driving Oracle's strategic acquisitions and financial stability.

- Leadership in Tech: Her leadership has positioned Oracle as a leader in cloud computing and enterprise technology.

Lisa Su - The Semiconductor Pioneer

- Innovation: Su's focus on high-performance computing and semiconductor innovation has driven AMD's resurgence.

- Resilience: Her ability to navigate industry challenges and drive long-term growth is a testament to her resilience and strategic vision.

Rosalind Brewer - The Retail Trailblazer

- Customer-Centric Innovation: Brewer's focus

on enhancing customer experience and driving digital transformation has been key to her success in retail.

- Diversity and Inclusion: Her commitment to diversity and inclusion has strengthened organizational culture and performance.

Common Themes: Identifying Recurring Themes in Their Success Stories

While each of these female leaders has a unique story, several common themes emerge that highlight the qualities and strategies that have contributed to their success.

1. Innovation and Adaptability

Innovation is a recurring theme in the success stories of these leaders. Whether through product innovation, marketing strategies, or business models, these women have continuously pushed the boundaries and brought new ideas to the market. Their ability to adapt to changing environments and embrace new technologies has also been crucial.

2. Strategic Vision and Leadership

Each leader exhibited a strong strategic vision for their companies. They set clear goals and priorities, communicated effectively, and inspired their teams to achieve common objectives. Their strategic leadership has driven growth, navigated challenges, and positioned their companies for long-term success.

3. Empowerment and Mentorship

Empowering others has been a cornerstone of their leadership styles. Whether it's Mary Kay Ash's support for her sales force, Oprah Winfrey's mentorship of emerging talents, or Indra Nooyi's focus on developing future leaders, these women have invested in building strong, supportive communities.

4. Customer-Centric Approach

A focus on understanding and meeting customer needs has been pivotal. These leaders prioritized delivering exceptional customer experiences, personalizing interactions, and building strong customer relationships. This customer-centric approach has driven loyalty, growth, and brand strength.

5. Resilience and Persistence

Resilience in the face of challenges and persistence in pursuing their goals are common traits. These leaders navigated financial difficulties, industry competition, and personal setbacks with determination and strategic thinking.

6. Diversity and Inclusion

Promoting diversity and inclusion has been a priority for many of these leaders. They have championed initiatives to create more inclusive workplaces, supported underrepresented groups, and leveraged diversity to drive innovation and organizational success.

7. Philanthropy and Social Impact

Using their success to make a positive impact on society has been a shared value. Whether through philanthropic efforts, corporate social responsibility initiatives, or advocacy for social causes, these leaders have demonstrated a commitment to giving back and driving positive change.

Future Outlook: The Evolving Role of Women in Business and Entrepreneurship

The role of women in business and entrepreneurship is evolving, with increasing opportunities and recognition for female leaders. Several trends and factors are shaping the future outlook for women in these fields.

Increasing Representation in Leadership Roles
The number of women in leadership positions is steadily increasing across industries. Efforts to promote gender diversity and inclusion, along with the success of trailblazing female leaders, are paving the way for more women to take on executive roles. Organizations are recognizing the value of diverse leadership teams in driving innovation and business performance.

Emphasis on Diversity and Inclusion

The emphasis on diversity and inclusion is becoming more pronounced. Companies are implementing policies and initiatives to ensure equal opportunities, address unconscious bias, and create inclusive cultures. This focus on diversity is driving positive change and enabling more women to thrive in business and entrepreneurship.

Supportive Networks and Mentorship

Supportive networks and mentorship programs are playing a crucial role in empowering women. Organizations, industry groups, and educational institutions are providing platforms for women to connect, share experiences, and support each other's professional growth. Mentorship from successful female leaders is helping to develop the next generation of women in business.

Access to Capital and Resources

Access to capital and resources is improving for female entrepreneurs. Venture capital firms, angel investors, and financial institutions are recognizing the potential of women-led businesses and increasing their support. Initiatives and programs aimed at providing funding, training, and resources to female entrepreneurs are helping to level the playing field.

Technological Advancements and Innovation

Technological advancements and innovation are creating new opportunities for women in business. The digital transformation of industries, the rise of e-commerce, and the proliferation of online platforms are enabling women to launch and scale businesses more easily. Women are leveraging technology to drive innovation, reach global markets, and disrupt traditional business models.

Changing Social Norms and Cultural Shifts

Changing social norms and cultural shifts are influencing the role of women in business. There is growing recognition of the importance of work-life balance, flexible working arrangements, and the need to address systemic barriers to gender equality. These cultural shifts are creating a more supportive environment for women to pursue careers in business and entrepreneurship.

Encouragement: Inspiring the Next Generation of Female Leaders

The stories and achievements of these female business leaders serve as powerful sources of inspiration for the next generation. Here are some key messages to inspire and empower future female leaders.

1. Embrace Innovation and Take Risks

Innovation often requires stepping out of your comfort zone and taking risks. Don't be afraid to challenge the status quo, explore new ideas, and pursue unconventional paths. Embrace a mindset of continuous learning and be open to new opportunities and experiences.

2. Develop a Clear Vision and Strategic Plan

Having a clear vision and strategic plan is essential for success. Define your goals, create a roadmap to achieve them, and communicate your vision effectively. Stay focused on your long-term objectives while remaining adaptable to changing circumstances.

3. Build Strong Networks and Seek Mentorship

Building strong networks and seeking mentorship are crucial for personal and professional growth. Surround yourself with supportive individuals who can provide guidance, share experiences, and offer opportunities. Mentorship from experienced leaders can provide valuable insights and help navigate challenges.

4. Prioritize Diversity and Inclusion

Promoting diversity and inclusion should be a priority in your leadership journey. Embrace diverse perspectives, create inclusive environments, and advocate for equal opportunities. Leveraging diversity will drive innovation, enhance team performance, and contribute to a more equitable workplace.

5. Stay Resilient and Persistent

Resilience and persistence are key traits of successful leaders. Stay focused on your goals, persevere through challenges, and learn from setbacks. Your ability to adapt, remain determined, and maintain a positive attitude will be instrumental in achieving success.

6. Give Back and Drive Social Impact

Use your success to make a positive impact on society. Engage in philanthropic efforts, support social causes, and advocate for positive change. Giving back to your community and driving social impact will not only enhance your legacy but also inspire others to follow in your footsteps.

7. Believe in Yourself and Your Potential

Believe in yourself and your potential to achieve greatness. Trust your abilities, embrace your strengths, and have confidence in your decisions. Remember that you have the power to shape your future and make a meaningful impact in the world.

The legacy of female business leaders like Estee Lauder, Mary Kay Ash, Oprah Winfrey, Martha Stewart, Meg Whitman, Sara Blakely, Indra Nooyi, Angela Ahrendts, Sheila Johnson, Safra Catz, Lisa Su, and Rosalind Brewer is a testament to the power of innovation, strategic vision, resilience, and advocacy for diversity. Their stories highlight the importance of embracing change, empowering others, and driving positive impact in their industries and communities.

As the role of women in business and entrepreneurship continues to evolve, the lessons and themes from these leaders will serve as a guiding light for future generations. By embracing innovation, developing strategic visions, prioritizing diversity, and staying resilient, the next generation of female leaders can build on the legacy of these trailblazers and create a more inclusive and successful future.

The journey of these remarkable women serves as an inspiration and a call to action for aspiring female leaders. Their achievements demonstrate that with determination, vision, and support, women can overcome barriers, drive innovation, and make lasting contributions to the business world. The future is bright for women in business, and the legacy of these leaders will continue to inspire and shape the path for generations to come.

www.ingramcontent.com/pod-product-compliance
Lightning Source LLC
Chambersburg PA
CBHW071910210526
45479CB00002B/362